COPYRIGHT

Advertising Under One Hour
By Laurence Minsky

Copyright © 2018 Under One Hour, LLC

Published by Under One Hour, LLC 2012-2018

Discover other titles by Under One Hour at www.UnderOneHour.com

This book is available in print at most online retailers.

Createspace Edition, License Notes

This book is licensed for your personal enjoyment only. This book may not be re-sold or given away to other people. If you would like to share this book with another person, please purchase an additional copy for each recipient. If you're reading this book and did not purchase it, or it was not purchased for your use only, then please return to your favorite book retailer and purchase your own copy. Thank you for respecting the hard work of this author.

ADDITIONAL PRAISE FOR ADVERTISING UNDER ONE HOUR

"An insightful read from Laurence Minsky, welcoming those new to the advertising field and also inspiring those long entrenched in it."

– Tracy Arrington, Author (with Matthew Fredrick), *101 Things I Learned in Advertising School* & Lecturer, Stan Richards School of Advertising and PR at the University of Texas at Austin

"Advertising in Under One Hour lives up to its title, offering a fast-paced, and utterly readable trip through the life and history of advertising. By knowing what advertising was and once meant, we can imagine what advertising will always mean, and how it will be used in the future. Because of the book's clear and comprehensive content, *Advertising in Under One Hour* would be a suitable textbook for an advertising or marketing communications course or a supplement for courses on principles or branding."

– David Aron, Professor of Marketing, Brennan School of Business, Dominican University

"A good reminder of all the things I assume everyone in the industry knows that most probably don't.

– Thomas Kemeny, copywriter, author of *Junior: Writing Your Way Ahead in Advertising* (Spring 2019 from powerHouse Books)

"It takes one hour for Mr. Minsky to clearly define the main ingredients necessary in creating award-winning advertising. Also, a great read for someone just entering the field."

– Alan Rado, MFA, Professor-College of DuPage & Owner & Creative Director, Adrado

ALSO BY LAURENCE MINSKY

The Activation Imperative: How to Build Brands by Inspiring Action
(with William Rosen)

Audio Branding: Using Sound to Build Your Brand
(with Colleen Fahey)

The Get A Job Workshop: How to Find Your Way to a Creative Career in Advertising, Branding, Collateral, Digital, Experiential & More
(as Executive Editor)

How to Succeed in Advertising When All You Have Is Talent
(Second Edition)

"All advertising advertises advertising."

—Marshall McLuhan

McLuhan, Marshall. (2003) *Understanding Media: The Extensions of Man Critical Edition*. Gingko Press. (Also included in *The Book of Probes*, Gingko Press.) Used with permission.

ACKNOWLEDGMENTS

A book can't be written without the support of others. Special thanks to: Dave Aron, Tracy Arrington, Michael Babcock, Bruce Bendinger, Andrew Brown, Christina Buczek, Kevin Christopheren, Ben DiSanti, Eric Freedman, Patrick Herron, David Houle, Michael Jolls, Thomas Kemeny, Dr. Kwang-Wu Kim, Bryan Mattimore, Mary Mattucci, Suzanne McBride, Tim McLaughlin, Margaret Murphy, Alan Rado, William Rosen, Craig Sigele, Traecy Smith, Stanley Wearden, and the Columbia College Sabbatical Committee for enabling me to write this piece, as well as, of course, my family and all of the baristas who kept me well caffeinated.

DEDICATION

To David Abbott, Carl Ally, Ralph Ammirati, Ron Anderson, Dana Arnett, Bruce Barton, Don Beldin, Bruce Bendinger, Bill Bernbach, Marcel Bleustein-Blanchet, Alex Bogusky, Rick Boyko, Leo Burnett, Tom Burrell, Leo Burnett, Elmo Calkins, John Caples, Steve Cartozian, Jay Chiat, Lee Clow, Tim Delaney, Jerry Della Femina, Ernest Dictor, Ben DiSanti, Ned Doyle, Jim Durfee, Phil Dusenberry, Don Easdon, Colleen Fahey, Mark Fenske, Bernice Fitz-Gibbon, Bud Frankel, Cliff Freeman, Emerson Foote, Benjamin Franklin, Bob Gage, Amil Gargano, Susan Gillette, Jeffrey Goodby, Howard Gossage, Roy Grace, Paula Green, Bob Greenberg, Tom Hamilton. Marion Harper, Jr, Steve Hayden, John Hegarty, Jelly Helm, Ken Hicks, Claude Hopkins, Susan Hoffman, Mike Hughes, Harry Jacobs, Linda Kaplan Thaler, David Kennedy, John E. Kennedy, Janet Kestin, Mike Koelker, Julian Koenig, Alex Kroll, Helmut Krone, Albert Lasker, Bob Levenson, George Lois, David Lubars, James Lucas, Theordore F. MacManus, Jane Maas, Ed McCabe, Tom McElligott, Anna Morris, Washington Olivetto, David Ogilvy, Alex Osborn, Shirley Polykoff, Martin Puris, Paul Rand, Rosser Reeves, Helen Landsdowne Resor, Stanley Resor, Nancy Rice, Stan Richards, Hal Riney, Jim Riswold, Phyllis Robinson, William Rosen, Diane Rothschild, Raymond Rubicam, Sam Scali, William Sharp, Rich Silverstein, Luke Sullivan, Rory Sutherland, Mike Tesch, J. Walter Thompson, David Trott, Nancy Vonk, James Webb Young, Mary Wells Lawrence, Dan Wieden, Tracy Wong, James Young Webb, Lester Wunderman, and all of the other leaders who changed the industry – while I only met a few of them, I learned from all of them – and, of course, to Rhonda and Jorie, who both changed me for the better. Finally, in memory of Millie, my faithful friend who kept me company as I wrote the manuscript.

TABLE OF CONTENTS

Note: Approximate Length in time is determined by
the average US reading speed of 300 words per minute.

I.	<u>Forward</u>	15
II.	<u>Introduction</u>	17

1. <u>What is Advertising:</u>
<u>An Overview & Brief History</u> (First 10 Minutes) — 19

- Advertising: A Working Definition — 20
- America's Earliest Advertising – And Advertising Practitioners — 23
- Kennedy and Lasker — 26
- A Roadmap to the Remaining Content — 31

2. <u>A Look at How it Works:</u>
<u>Hard Sell, Soft Sell, & More</u> (Second 10 Minutes) — 33

- What is a Brand — 36
- What's Your Point of View? — 37
- Know What you Believe — 38
- Advertising's Three Levels of Ethical Questions — 39
- Subliminal Messages — 42
- The Goal of Advertising Revisited — 43

3. <u>Strategic Development:</u>
<u>Ready, Aim, Insights & Fire</u> (Third 10 Minutes) — 45

- The Four Key Tools of Marketing — 46
- To Increase the Price, Change the Packaging — 47
- Pre-Emption, USP, & Positioning — 47
- Welcome to Account Planning — 49
- A Newer Position Within the Industry — 50
- Account Planning Sixty Years Later — 52
- Some Insights on Generating Insights — 53
- Briefs Should be Brief — 54
- Future Reading: The Fields That Contribute to Advertising Insights — 55

4. <u>Let's Get Creative: Copy,</u>
<u>Art Direction, & Production</u> (Fourth 10 Minutes) — 57

- A Marriage Counselor For Creatives — 57
- The Element of an Ad Message — 59
- The Hierarchy of Your Message — 60
- Soak Up Ideas & Write Them Down — 61
- Advertising Shouldn't Sound Like Advertising — 62
- Tell Your Story — 63
- Some Key Considerations When Creating Advertising — 65
- See & Say is Not the Solution — 65
- Be Open to Breaking the Rules — 66

5. **Your True Message:**
   Media Choices & Media Channels (Fifth 10 Minutes)   **69**
   - ➤ The Context is the Message, Too   70
   - ➤ Media Bought & Sold   71
   - ➤ Developing the Plan   72
   - ➤ Options, Options, Options   73
   - ➤ What More Can You Get?   76
   - ➤ Programmatic Can Be Problematic   77
   - ➤ Back to Advertising's Roots   78

6. **Onward: Analysis,**
   Agency Selection, & Next Steps (Final 10 Minutes)   **81**
   - ➤ It's a Decision-Making Business   82
   - ➤ What Should Clients Seek in an Agency   83
   - ➤ What Do Agencies Seek in a Client?   84
   - ➤ Ad Agencies: The Profit Part   85
   - ➤ Estimating, Approximately Speaking   87
   - ➤ A Look to the Future   88
   - ➤ A Little Knowledge Goes a Short Way   89

7. **Bibliography**   **95**

8. **Index/Key Terms**   **99**

9. **About the Author**   **101**

FOREWORD

My dad, J. Clark "Matti" Mattimore, was one of the original "Mad Men." He created, for instance, the highly-strategic tag line, "Say, Pepsi Please" to counter the common expression "Gimme a Coke." From my dad, I learned both the thinking processes that went into creating a great ad, as well as a love for "the big idea."

Fresh out of college with a degree in psychology, I worked in advertising for a short time. Then, later on, I taught advertising executives and clients how to use simple ideation techniques to generate bigger and better ideas. Today, my innovation agency works with dozens of ad agencies to position and launch new products and services for our clients.

So frankly, given my background in advertising, marketing, strategy, product positioning, qualitative market research, branding and idea creation, I wasn't sure Larry's book would have much, if anything, to offer me.

Wrong!

Somehow, Larry has been able to distill 140 years of advertising history, and best-thinking practices in the creation of great advertising, into a 59-minute read. Some of what Larry has written I knew before but was happy to be reminded of. But there was much new as well.

So, you can spend literally decades learning the foundational principles and practice of creating great advertising. Or, you can spend the next now 58 minutes taking a crash course in what's MOST important to know about advertising. Your choice, of course, but the clock is ticking.

Bryan Mattimore
Cofounder and Chief Idea Guy, Growth Engine
Author, *21 Days to a Big Idea*

THE GROWTH ENGINE CO.

INTRODUCTION

Welcome to the world of advertising, something that has been part of your life as long as you can remember. It's both business and entertainment. It saturates our society and draws from cultural truths.

If you're practically minded, you might be asking how can I use advertising to get more customers for my business? Or, if it sounds like a career for you, what are the opportunities?

In this little book, you're also going to learn about this fascinating business. You'll meet some of the key players in the industry and the innovations that brought them success. You'll also learn some of the key strategies and the process for creating advertising.

We'll begin with a quick review of some of advertising's interesting history. Then we'll show you the process or steps for creating effective advertising as well as analyzing the results. Throughout, we'll also cover the roles and responsibilities of the various professionals who work in the field and include some basic definitions. As a final bonus, I offer recommendations and resources at the end for those who want to learn more.

I hope you enjoy Advertising Under One Hour. It was written in a conversational tone, just like advertising. Plus, it can help you if you are:

- Interested in joining the field – this overview should give you a basis for figuring where you fit and what you need to do to get started.
- A marketer who wants to work with an agency – the following pages should give you a foundation for understanding how they work and how you can get more out of them.
- A small business owner – this should give you a process for creating your own ads and give you a basis for judging them and their effectiveness.

Whatever your goals, I hope you enjoy this hour of discovery. It's not a lot of time, so let's get started. And if you have an extra few minutes after, please do me a favor: send me your comments, questions, and reactions; getting feedback is one of the ways we all get better.

Thank you.

WHAT IS ADVERTISING: AN OVERVEIW & BRIEF HISTORY

(FIRST 10 MINUTES)

Love it or hate it, advertising is one of those professions where everyone seems to know what it is when they see it, but, surprisingly, few seem to be able to agree on a solid definition of it.

However, some advertising does have consistent characteristics.

First, **message control.** The sponsor of the advertisement has complete control over the message, unlike in public relations, which seeks to influence others, namely the media, but also bloggers and other online influencers, to deliver the intended message to the ultimate audience.

Second, it's a **paid message.** The place – or medium – where the advertising appears is typically bought from a publisher or broadcaster such as time on a television or radio station ("internet" TV and radio included) or space in a print/online magazine, social media platform, on an outdoor billboard, and within purchased environments such as on the floor of a grocery store.

The advertising could also appear in a medium "**owned**" by the advertiser, such as their website, blog, or in flyers and brochures they distribute themselves. The definition also includes direct mailings, but in a sense the postal service serves as the medium since they deliver the messages.

Third, the people who run ads are seeking to achieve an objective. Advertising is **communication with a purpose.** There are numerous possible objectives. Some of the more common goals include:

- **Awareness.** To let the target audience(s) know about the existence of the product, service, and/or person (usually a politician, but could be a celebrity, fashion designer, or someone else).
- **Persuasion.** To change the audience's mind about the advertised product, service, or idea (often called repositioning the product or service) or vote for a politician.
- **"Word-of-mouth."** To inspire people to talk to others about what is being advertised or, more likely, the advertising itself.
- **Trial.** To persuade the audience(s) to try or buy a product or service, adopt an idea, or take some other desired action.
- **Reminder.** Simply reminding the audience(s) that the product or service still exists (reinforcement of prior beliefs), so they remember to re-purchase it and build loyalty to it.

ADVERTISING: A WORKING DEFINITION

One definition I particularly like is from Robert Cluley in his book *Essentials of Advertising*: ads "are attempts to change demand through communication."[1]

A refinement to that definition might be that ads are attempts at increasing demand of the featured product, service, or idea through some form of media communication.

---

[1] Cluley, Robert. (2017) *Essentials of Advertising*. London, Kogan Page.

Earlier definitions contributed to this understanding. For instance, John E. Kennedy, a turn-of-the-century ad writer discussed later in this chapter, presented the definition that advertising is "salesmanship in print" back around 1905.[2]

While slightly dated for obvious reasons, this definition advanced our understanding of advertising's job by suggesting that an ad message should persuade its audience to take action, rather than merely provide information, which was the prevailing paradigm.

Of course, there are many exceptions. It may be that the ad merely features information and that is enough to achieve its goals. Ads announcing sales are primarily informational, although the more effective examples also create a strong sense of urgency, so the intended audience will feel the need to "act now" or miss out.

Whatever the definition one adopts, the ad should create a benefit for the company running it. In fact, the practice of advertising probably wouldn't have such a long history if it hadn't at least intuitively achieved some form of its commercial objectives for those sponsoring the messaging.

Advertising dates back to some of our earliest history. Poster advertising dating back to 2000 BC in Egypt has been reported. Advertising on papyrus was used across ancient Greece and Rome. Tourists in Pompeii can spot a well-preserved not-safe-for-work ad from 79 AD promoting the world's oldest profession.[3]

The early practice of advertising can be found in other parts of the globe as well. In China, for instance, between the 11th and 7th centuries BC, ads were often conveyed through words and music. One of the earliest

---

[2] I've heard that he wasn't the first to come up with this definition, but it appears that his use of it was the first time it stuck within the industry.
[3] History of advertising: No. 142, Campaign, July, 20, 2015
https://www.campaignlive.co.uk/article/history-advertising-no-142-pompeii-penis/1357977 [Accessed: 21, June, 2018].

known examples of advertising: a printing plate in China from the Song Dynasty (960 –1297 AD)[4] promoting a sewing needle shop.[5]

In Europe, during the Middle Ages, shop owners put up signs and used barkers to call people to their shops. Then, the technology of the printing press added new opportunities – with handbills, flyers, and newspapers.[6]

One of the biggest growth spurts in advertising occurred as mass manufacturing, mass media, mass distribution, and mass education took root.[7] [8] Some argue that it's because we needed the confluence of goods to sell, places to promote them (the media), places to buy them, and a basic level of literacy for advertising to become an effective strategy.[9]

During this time, with the growth of department stores,[10] manufacturers were becoming separated from the people buying their products and advertising was seen as a way to bridge the gap, replacing direct sales.

---

[4] Song Dynasty. (2017) *Wikipedia*. [Online] Available from: https://en.wikipedia.org/wiki/Song_dynasty [Accessed 3 October 2017].
[5] VandeWaa, David, The Ancient Origins and History of Modern Marketing and Advertising. (2016) *LaFleur*. [Online] Available from: https://lafleur.marketing/blog/ancient-origins-history-modern-marketing-advertising/ [Accessed 15 July 2018].
[6] The Ancient Origins and History of Modern Marketing and Advertising. (2016) *LaFleur*. [Online] Available from: https://lafleur.marketing/blog/ancient-origins-history-modern-marketing-advertising/ [Accessed 19 December 2017].
[7] History: 19th Century. (2003) *AdAge*. [Online] Available from: http://adage.com/article/adage-encyclopedia/history-19th-century/98706/ [Accessed 19 December 2017].
[8] Bendinger, Bruce et al (2009) *Advertising & The Business of Brands Fourth (Media Revolution) Edition*, Chicago, IL: The Copy Workshop.
[9] Bendinger, Bruce et al (2009) *Advertising & The Business of Brands Fourth (Media Revolution) Edition*, Chicago, IL: The Copy Workshop.
[10] History: 19th Century. (2003) *AdAge*. [Online] Available from: http://adage.com/article/adage-encyclopedia/history-19th-century/98706/ [Accessed 19 December 2017].

AMERICA'S EARLIEST ADVERTISING – AND ADVERTISING PRACTITIONERS

Ben Franklin was one of America's first advertising professionals. He was even inducted into the Advertising Hall of Fame for his pioneering efforts. According to his inscription, Franklin sold "products and services, community programs, democracy, and America itself."[11]

Franklin was among the first to set empty space around the advertisement, so they'd pop out and use headlines to grab attention as well as images – in his case, wood cuts – to telegraph the ad contents.[12]

An example of early American advertising.
Source: Varsity Tutors, Archiving Early America
https://www.varsitytutors.com/earlyamerica/rare-images/early-day-ads.

---

[11] Advertising Hall of Fame, American Advertising Federation. [Online] Available from: http://advertisinghall.org/members/member_bio.php?memid=632 [Accessed September 15, 2017].

[12] Applegate, Edd (2012) *The Rise of Advertising in the United States: A History of Innovation to 1960*, Lanham, MD, Scarecrow Press.

One suggestion that Franklin reportedly gave to those taking out advertisements in his newspaper was to: "underestimate the quality of their goods so as to impress a buyer with its unexpected merit."[13] "Under-promise and over-deliver" is a suggestion that can still work today – particularly in light of social media where advertisers want to delight users so that the users give positive reviews.

Advertising agencies began popping up around 1790 in London. At first, they represented the newspapers and their job was to sell advertising space.[14] **Volney B. Palmer** is considered to be America's first advertising agent. While selling real estate in Philadelphia, he expanded his portfolio to include coal and by 1842, advertising space.[15] The model then evolved and in this new one, the advertising agency would buy all of the advertising space in a publication, break it into smaller blocks, and resell it for a markup in price.[16] In this model, the agent was essentially a middleman.[17]

The model changed again in 1869 when **Francis W. Ayer** started an agency. Since he was only twenty at the time – advertising has always been a young person's business – he decided it would be easier to sell the ad space if he named the firm after his dad – **N.W. Ayer & Son**.

His first change: rather than selling advertising space, his agency became a space buyer, taking a commission from the purchase as his profit. By buying ad space rather than selling it, Ayer felt he could better represent

---

[13] Advertising Hall of Fame, American Advertising Federation, [Online] Available from: http://advertisinghall.org/members/member_bio.php?memid=632 [Accessed September 15, 2017].
[14] History of Advertising No 84: The World's First Ad Agency. (2013) *Campaign*. [Online] Available from: https://www.campaignlive.co.uk/article/history-advertising-no-84-worlds-first-ad-agency/1220515#GPeHIsIffbjb3OG4.99 [Accessed 19 December 2017].
[15] Early Advertising. (2011) *Graphic Design History*. [Online] Available from: http://www.designhistory.org/Advertising_pages/FirstAd.html [Accessed 19 December 2017].
[16] History: 19th Century. (2003) *AdAge*. [Online] Available from: http://adage.com/article/adage-encyclopedia/history-19th-century/98706/ [Accessed 19 December 2017].
[17] History: 19th Century. (2003) *AdAge*. [Online] Available from: http://adage.com/article/adage-encyclopedia/history-19th-century/98706/ [Accessed 19 December 2017].

the needs of his clients. Around 1880, the agency started rejecting "advertising that would discredit the agency or disappoint the advertiser."[18]

The agency's two other major innovations: an annual **advertising plan** for each client, based on market surveys and copywriting services, effectively making NW Ayer & Son the first **full-service agency** – a firm that offered account services, market research, creative services (copywriting, art direction, and design), and media planning and buying.

In many ways, these additional services essentially acted as "loss leaders," which is when a company provides a service or product for free or below cost to sell other, more profitable items or services later. In this case, full-service agencies would offer the above services for free when pitching the advertiser to get them to buy ad space through them, which is how agencies made their money, a legacy that some would argue is still hurting the industry today.[19]

Meanwhile, another industry advancement came from **P.T. Barnum**. While he was more known for showmanship and his skills at generating publicity by getting newspapers to publish articles about himself and his "properties" – including his museum, circus, and the shows he produced – he also brought the practice of creating campaigns to advertising, generating

---

[18] History: 19th Century. (2003) *AdAge*. [Online] Available from: http://adage.com/article/adage-encyclopedia/history_19th-century/98706/ [Accessed 19 December 2017].

[19] Giving away key services such as research and creative development during a pitch devalues the insights, ideas, knowledge, and skills that make the advertising effective. In fact, creative services were not "professionalized" until the 1970s.[19] And many agencies still give away their insights, ideas, strategies, and creative messaging when they are trying to land new clients. As a result, they often hide these costs in the billings for other clients or provide lesser examples that might sound compelling during presentations but are not quite as effective in the marketplace. A more productive route is to look at the agency's track record of creating effective, unique solutions for their other clients, which we'll explore in the following chapters. Information on the professionalization of the industry can be found in Minsky, Laurence. & Peters, Julia Tang. (2015) How You Make Decisions Is as Important as What You Decide. Harvard Business Review. [Online] Available from: https://hbr.org/2015/04/how-you-make-decisions-is-as-important-as-what-you-decide [Accessed 19 December 2017].

different but coordinated messages all with the same idea or message and objective.[20]

KENNEDY AND LASKER

Remember John E. Kennedy who defined advertising as "salesmanship in print"? Already a successful copywriter in Canada, he changed the shape of advertising by forwarding a note to the owners of a Chicago-based agency, Lord & Thomas, inviting them to meet him at the bar in the lobby of their office building so he could explain advertising. The owners passed, but a junior member of the agency, **Albert Lasker**, took him up on the offer. Lasker reportedly defined advertising as "news" at which Kennedy provided his now famous definition. Impressed, Lasker offered him a job to write an ad copy for the agency, pioneering the use of "reason why" advertising – i.e., providing an explicit rationale or point for buying the product. Kennedy used coupons to test the effectiveness of his ads by comparing the response rates, a method which is still effective today.

Lasker was another character. As his story goes, he was originally from Galveston, Texas starting in journalism at the age of 12 when he launched his own newspaper. After graduating from high school, he started working full-time for *Galveston Daily News* – he'd written for them earlier – and was assigned to write the review for the local premier of a new opera. However, he had prior plans for that night and knew the opera's story, so he wrote his "review" earlier in the day without seeing the production and filed it with his editor.

---

[20] Applegate, Edd (2012) *The Rise of Advertising in the United States: A History of Innovation to 1960*, Lanham, MD, Scarecrow Press.

As timing would have it, the opera house burned down before the premier. Knowing his credibility was ruined, he left town and, eventually, left journalism.

His father suggested advertising and introduced him to Daniel Lord, owner of Lord & Thomas, who then hired him at $10 a week. Soon, however, Lasker ran into another problem: he lost $500 gambling. Since Lord paid his debt, Lasker knew that he needed to stick around for a bit and decided to dedicate himself to building a career. It was then that he hired Kennedy.

After Kennedy, Lasker, who was in charge of the copy department, hired **Claude Hopkins**, who invented the concept of "**pre-emptive" advertising** – taking an intrinsic fact all competitors could claim and being the first to use it to promote a brand. Hopkins books, especially *Scientific Advertising*, are still required reading by many today.

The ad that launched the creative revolution. The body copy was rewritten after it first ran and the example you see here contains the second, revised version.

There were, of course, other notable characters throughout the history of advertising. In the post-war 1950s, a time that emphasized conformity, ad legend **David Ogilvy** used to show up at society events in New York wearing a kilt. He inherently understood the need to stand out and get noticed, another factor for successful advertising. Designer **Paul Rand** came up with the idea of matching an art director with a copywriter to conceive the ad.[21] He told the idea to his young copywriter, **Bill Bernbach**, who used it when forming his agency, **Doyle Dane Bernbach** (DDB).

By creating a marriage of words and pictures and focusing on a "concept" for each ad, among other advances, DDB ushered in the creative revolution of the 1960s and brought the world many legendary admen and stories about the industry that are still told today. n one story, **George Lois**, the alleged model for Don Draper – a claim rejected by Lois, who says he was more talented than the *Mad Men* lead – threatened to jump out a window when a client wouldn't buy an ad; apparently, the threat worked, because the ad ran and Lois never jumped.[22]

---

[21] According to the *Copy Workshop Workbook*, Rand was not the only one to come up with the idea of matching copywriters with art directors; Young and Rubicon used this method before DDB (I also have to imagine that Rand used it at the agency where he was creative director too). The difference was that DDB popularized it.

[22] Lunch With George Lois. (2001) *AdAge*. [Online] Available from: http://adage.com/article/people-players/lunch-george-lois/92517/ [Accessed 27 December 2017].

Era	Key Advancement	Key Player(s)
1720s	Birth of advertising in America	Ben Franklin
1850s	The first ad "campaign"	PT Barnum
1870s	The first full-service ad agency	N. W. Ayer & Son / Francis Ayer
1900s	Reason-why advertising	John Kennedy/Albert Lasker
1910s	Pre-emptive advertising	Claude Hopkins
	Sex appeal in advertising	Helen Landowne-Resor
1920s	Testimonial advertising	Helen Landowne-Resor
1930s	Event marketing	Bernice Fitz-Gibbon
1940s	Inherent drama	Leo Burnett *
1950s	Unique selling proposition (USP)	Rosser Reeves **
1960s	The creative revolution / big idea	Bill Bernbach
	Emotional persuasion (classy & smart)	David Ogilvy

1970s	Positioning	Jack Trout & Al Reis
	Comparative advertising	Carl Ally, Amil Gargano (Carl Ally Inc)
1980s	Brand image advertising	Jay Chiat & Lee Clow (Chiat + Day)
1990s	Post-modern (self-referential, ironic)	Dan Wiedon (Wiedon + Kennedy)
	Brand marketing (promotions)	Bud Frankel (Frankel & Company)
2000s	Viral marketing	Alex Bogusky (CP+B)
2010s	Brand activation	William Rosen (VSA Partners) ***

* While most associate the agency with their critters of the 1950s and 1960s, the agency was started in 1935 and, from what I can tell, Leo Burnett's concept of inherent drama was already established by the 1940s.

** While pioneered in the 1940s, the concept of USP is often associated with early television advertising, which was also pioneered by Rosser Reeves.

*** While we are still in this decade, I believe it will be considered the era of brand activation, which is why William Rosen of VSA Partners and I wrote the book "The Activation Imperative: How to Build Brand and Business by Inspiring Action."

Another important figure is **Leo Burnett.** His Chicago agency focused on conveying the "inherent drama" of the brands they advertised, expressing the single factor "about that product that keeps it in the marketplace."[23] In other words, they would dramatize the product's reason for being. The Green Giant, the Marlboro cowboy, Kellogg's Cereal characters (like Tony the Tiger), and the Poppin' Fresh Doughboy all came out of the Leo Burnett agency.

A ROADMAP TO THE REMAINING CONTENT

The theme of this chapter has been that advertising is a driver of commerce. However, even today, in the era of big data and technology-enabled testing, most advertising is actually not as effective as it could be. Department store pioneer John Wannamaker once purportedly said, "Half the money I spend on advertising is wasted; the trouble is I don't know which half."[24] (I suspect that if 50% of his advertising spending was achieving its goals, then he had an unusually high batting average.)

Another way to look at it, according to ad legend Bruce Bendinger, is that "advertising is a business of spectacular exceptions." And everyone in it is working to be the creator of one of the exceptions that are spectacularly successful.

---

[23] Higgins, Dennis (2203) *The Art of Writing Advertising: Conversations with Masters of the Craft: David Ogilvy, William Bernbach, Leo Burnett, Rosser Reeves*," New York: McGraw Hill Advertising Age Classics Library

[24] Bullmore, Jeremy (2013) WPP Annual Report & Accounts 2013 [Online] "Why it's Time to Say Goodbye to IKTHTMISOAIW* (*I know that half the money I spend on advertising is wasted ...) http://www.wpp.com/annualreports/2013/what-we-think/why-its-time-to-say-goodbye-to-ikthtmisoaiw/ [Accessed 20 January 2018].

But it doesn't have to be this way.

There are strategies, processes, and principles for creating effective advertising. We'll cover some of them in the remaining chapters.

A LOOK AT HOW IT WORKS: HARD SELL, SOFT SELL, & MORE (SECOND 10 MINUTES)

Just as the definition of advertising varies widely, there is also a debate on how it works (if it even works) and its effect on our economy. One view states that advertising aims to make people like the brand, and if they like it they will buy it.[25] The purchase of a product or service is not a rational decision, but an emotional one, built on years of advertising, making it harder for potential competitors to enter the market. Some call this softer approach **pull advertising**.[26]

---

[25] Minsky, Laurence. (2007) *How to Succeed in Advertising When All You Have Is Talent*. Chicago, The Copy Workshop.

[26] Bendinger, Bruce et al (2009) *Advertising & The Business of Brands Fourth (Media Revolution) Edition*, Chicago, IL: The Copy Workshop.

An example of a Claude Hopkins-penned ad based on the idea of Albert Lasker, who came up with the idea of drinking orange juice on a regular basis when farmers couldn't sell all of their oranges.

In the opposite view, ads focus on features and benefits, on logical information about the brand – the "reason why" approach from Chapter 1. Even if it is just a sentence or a fragment, the message provides a nugget of *why* the prospect should buy the product. Proponents see consumers as generally making rational decisions and advertising provides the facts purchasers need to select the best product or service for them – or for bigger purchases, provide part of the information. Some people call this harder selling approach **push advertising**.[27]

Written in 1926 by John Caples one year into his career, this ad is considered to be one of the most successful ever. Its structure, especially the way the headline was written, has been used as the model for creating some of the most effective viral content on the web.

---

[27] Bendinger, Bruce et al (2009) *Advertising & The Business of Brands Fourth (Media Revolution) Edition*, Chicago, IL: The Copy Workshop.

Those who see people as active seekers of information, by extension, see advertising as an effective tool for launching new products or services, giving marketers the ability for them to get noticed. At the very least, the ad gets people to try the product or service, and if it is better in some way, it might replace the existing brand and could even become the leader.[28]

WHAT IS A BRAND?

According to Stan Richards, Chairman of The Richards Group (the agency who created and still produce the long-running Motel 6 radio campaign, among other great advertising), "A brand is a promise."[29] Or as Amazon boss Jeff Bezos purportedly once said, "A brand is what they say about you when you're not in the room."[30]

The goal of any brand-building effort is to put out the consistent signals that will make people think of the product or service in a way the marketer wants it to be perceived. The brand-building effort enables the product or service to differentiate itself, a key goal as more and more products in a given category are becoming very similar, e.g., most cars in a class have the same features and offer the same functional benefits. It is the branding that sets them apart. The value these positive perceptions create is called **brand equity**.

---

[28] It is important to note, however, that the advertising approach for launching new products can also be more emotional and image-oriented. Think about many of the Apple product launches, for example.

[29] Minsky, Laurence. & Bendinger, Bruce. (2007) *How to Succeed in Advertising When All You Have Is Talent*. Chicago, The Copy Workshop.

[30] Effective Edge. (2018) *Five Pathways to Transformation*. [Online] Available from: http://effectiveedge.com/2016/02/your-brand-is-what-people-say-about-you-when-youre-not-in-the-room-jeff-bezos-founder-of-amazon/ [Accessed 19 December 2017].

Which brings us back to our main question: Does advertising enable new products and services to break through, get noticed, and displace the category leader? Or does it block out the ability of new products and services to break into the category?

Both have some truth, and the proponents on either side can find examples to support their views. A strong message can break through and help introduce an innovation that changes the category. Meanwhile, stronger brands can charge more[31] while their customers seem to be more loyal to them.[32] There are times when a feature-benefit-oriented hard-sell works and other times when an image-oriented soft-sell approach is more effective.

WHAT'S YOUR POINT OF VIEW?

How you should proceed – the use of advertising or not and, if so, hard sell or soft – depends on the situation. Determining the answer is one of the reasons advertising professionals can make big money (even though I've found the individual bias of practitioners regularly gets in the way of offering the best advice). But one thing a marketer probably shouldn't do is mix hard sell and soft sell in a single ad.

Yet you can see this all of the time. For example, on Hulu, I have been getting a commercial for a pet store. It opens on a dog talking about the stock market. Cute. But the spot then cuts to an explanation of the store's features and benefits, making it seem as if I am viewing two different spots. I feel

---

[31] Business Owner's Playbook. (2017) *Mature Business Marketing*. [Online] Available from: https://www.thehartford.com/business-playbook/in-depth/advantages-strong-brand-equity [Accessed 19 December 2017].

[32] Business Owner's Playbook. (2017) *Mature Business Marketing*. [Online] Available from: https://www.thehartford.com/business-playbook/in-depth/advantages-strong-brand-equity [Accessed 19 December 2017].

cheated and confused because I was hooked – or baited – by one approach and then it switched to another. While you can get both messages across in a broader campaign, it rarely works in the same piece of communication.

KNOW WHAT YOU BELIEVE

Two lessons here: If you're creating an ad, find and use the approach you believe in and seek clients who need it. As ad legend **Alex Bogusky** once said, "There's a certain genius to those screamer ads where people yell on the radio. I know people that do a lot of that stuff, and they believe in them – that it's the best way for the client to get a point across. Since they believe in that style, they're able to do it far better than I could, because I don't believe in them."[33]

And, if you are buying advertising, make sure that the people who are creating your ads believe in the approach that is best for your brand and situation. And whether you are a member of an agency, or green-lighting them as a marketer, you need to fully understand your bias and beliefs and make sure they align with the brand needs.

In other words, there is not a single, right formula – but there is a right formula for each brand.

The job of a marketer is to understand what approach is best for their brand. And the job of the agency is to recommend and deliver the best approach. This does not always happen! Often, consciously or unconsciously, agencies recommend the approach that brings them the best financial return, utilizes the approach they do best, or is the easiest to sell. Likewise,

---

[33] Minsky, Laurence (2007) *How to Succeed in Advertising When All You Have Is Talent*. Chicago, The Copy Workshop.

companies tend to either rely on the tried and true or jump to the "shiny new object" – the medium, tactic, style, or approach that is faddishly hot or was recently effective for a top brand or a direct competitor. Neither is healthy.

One way to keep individual biases – and agencies – in check is through what people in the industry call a "brief" – a short document outlining the assignment. We'll look more at brief development in the next chapter, but simply stated for now, the goal is to figure out what you want to achieve, which approach you need for achieving it, and where it should be seen.

ADVERTISING'S THREE LEVELS OF ETHICAL QUESTIONS

At the start of this chapter, I pointed out that people debate if advertising even works. And, it does. According to the Marketing Science Institute's book *Empirical Generalization About Marketing Impact*, edited by Dominique M. Hanssens, the answer is yes – when the situation is right, it can grow a business.[34]

Since advertising can change the behavior of its prospects, another area that practitioners should understand is their sense of ethics. Rory Sutherland, Vice Chairman, Ogilvy & Mather Group UK, once said, "If the creation of your advertising is not raising ethical questions, then you are not doing it right."[35]

Rory, of course, wasn't encouraging people to become unethical – just the opposite – he was calling attention to the importance of paying attention

---

[34] Hanssens, Dominique M. (2015) *Empirical Generalizations about Marketing Impact*. 2nd Ed. Cambridge, MA, Marketing Science Institute.
[35] Sutherland, Rory (2007) Unpublished email.

to your values, before the message has been brought to the marketplace. Part of the job during ad creation is to push the envelope, innovate, and explore new solutions. If a marketer just repeats what has been done, then the new ad won't be noticed. But if the proposed solution crosses ethical boundaries, it's the job of the marketer and agency professionals to stop it before it's distributed. Otherwise, it could hurt the brand (unless the brand stands for bad taste and questionable standards).

When discussing ethics within advertising, there tends to be three "buckets" or "levels:"[36]

1. **Societal**:
    a. Key questions:
        i. Should we even allow advertising?
        ii. If so, when should we allow it?
        iii. And, if so, what should we allow?

    b. Informing this discussion is the exploration of:
        i. What is advertising doing to us as a culture?
        ii. What is it doing to individuals and subgroups?
        iii. What is advertising's influence on media and what gets covered?

    c. Final consideration:
        i. Does advertising drive innovation because it informs the world about new products? Or,
        ii. Does it hinder innovation because it makes it harder for new products to get noticed?

2. **Corporate**:
    a. Key questions:
        i. How should an ad agency or client best operate?
            o What should they do when handed unduly obtained competitive information?
            o How should you treat employees? What is considered fair compensation?
        ii. What business practices should they follow?

---

[36] Spence, Edward H & Heekeren, Brett Van (2005) Advertising Ethics, Upper Saddle River, New Jersey, Pearson Prentice Hall

- Should they create work for free to win an account or use unpaid internship labor?
- Should they advertise to vulnerable audiences such as kids or seniors and, if so, how?
- Should the agency promote legal sin products or dangerous products such as guns, alcohol, and tobacco (and, if so, which of these categories)?
- Should they execute comparative advertising (and, if so, when and how)?

  b. Informing this discussion is the exploration of:
  i. What will help and what will cause harm to all the key stakeholders: prospects, clients, the business itself, and employees?
  ii. What are the standard industry practices? (These can and often change over time.)
  iii. What are the ethical guideposts of the business's management and of the employees? (See below.)

3. **Individual**:
   a. Key questions:
   i. How should I best operate; what are the practices and ethical choices I should make as a professional?
   ii. When do I take/claim and/or give credit?
   iii. What accounts am I willing to work on (e.g., my agency promotes "sin" products, but should I work on them and, if yes, which type or types)?
   iv. What do I do if I don't agree with the moral choices of my employer, colleagues, or client?
   v. What should I do if handed "insider" competitive information?
   vi. What should I expose during employment interviews?
   vii. How should I handle dinner with a supplier or potential supplier?
   - Do I share the cost of a $500 meal so I don't let colleagues think it influenced my decision or should I let him or her cover the check?

b. Informing this discussion is the exploration of:
    i. What are my personal ethical guideposts?
    ii. What are the ethical guideposts of management and my organization's values and do I agree with them? (See above.)
    iii. What do I find right and wrong beyond my employment?
    iv. What kind of reputation do I want in the industry?
    v. Would I personally use the product or service if I were in the prospect group?

While this list of questions and considerations are not all inclusive, I believe you get the picture. On each of these levels, you should come to an understanding of your values and how you would handle these types of questions. Clearly knowing where your lines are drawn – your principles – will help you stay aligned with them.

SUBLIMINAL MESSAGES

One format that raises ethical questioning but doesn't seem to work is subliminal advertising. The belief that people are being strongly manipulated by unconscious messaging has been around since the late 1940s (and has been outlawed since the 1950s).[37] While a quick Google search shows that some examples of subliminal advertising do exist (intentionally created or not) and sensory marketing can affect behavior on an unconscious level[38] to help build brand perception,[39] burying provocative words or

---

[37] Player, Alex. (2016) How Marlboro, Coke and KFC Used Subliminal Advertising. *Campaign*. [Online] Available from: https://www.campaignlive.co.uk/article/marlboro-coke-kfc-used-subliminal-advertising/1383489 [Accessed 19 December 2017].

[38] Margalit, Liraz. Ph.D. (2017) Sensory Marketing; The Smell of Cinnamon That Made Me Buy. *Psychology Today*. [Online] Available from: https://www.psychologytoday.com/blog/behind-online-behavior/201701/sensory-marketing-the-smell-cinnamon-made-me-buy [Accessed 19th December 2017].

[39] Minsky, Laurence. & Fahey, Colleen. (2017) *Audio Branding: Using Sound to Build Your Brand*. London, Kogan Page.

images in the main image – what is traditionally called subliminal advertising – doesn't seem to make people do things they wouldn't normally do.[40]

In fact, many marketers can't even get people to act on "liminal" messages – i.e., conscious or explicit advertising – let alone on subliminal ones, so why spend your time hiding the word "sex" in a drink's ice cubes when you can get a better return developing advertising that people actually want to read or watch and talk about and, thus, persuade them to act?

In other words, it's better to focus on what matters and create powerful advertising that gets noticed, drives action, and builds the brand, rather than on creating messaging that merely makes people feel manipulated when discovered.

THE GOAL OF ADVERTISING REVISITED

As mentioned in Chapter 1, the goal of advertising is to change demand – for the better. But as advertising legend **Rosser Reeves** pointed out way back in his classic 1961 book, ***Reality in Advertising***, marketers shouldn't automatically credit their advertising when they see a boost in sales.[41] It could be the price, competitor issues, or something else that coincidentally caused the bump in sales. Likewise, they shouldn't automatically blame the campaign when sales don't improve. Some of the areas that can limit growth include price, distribution, sales force, and, of course, the product itself.[42]

---

[40] Zimmerman, Ian. Ph.D. (2014) Subliminal Ads, Unconscious Influence, and Consumption: What Myths and Realities Surround Subliminal Ads, and What Does it Mean for You? *Psychology Today*. [Online] Available from: https://www.psychologytoday.com/blog/sold/201406/subliminal-ads-unconscious-influence-and-consumption [Accessed 7 November 2017].
[41] Reeves, Rosser. (2015) *Reality in Advertising*. Widener Classics.
[42] Reeves, Rosser. (2015) *Reality in Advertising*. Widener Classics.

Finally, as Reeves also pointed out, an ad or campaign could change demand – but in the wrong direction, decreasing sales.[43] It might be off-point, or might present a break in the brand voice, personality, or promise; it also might not reach the right audience. Or it might just turn people away, rightly or not, because it communicates that the product or service is not for them.[44]

But, of course, just as with boosting sales, don't be quick to blame the advertising. The downturn could also be a result of a competitive action, pricing and distribution issues, or another cause.

With marketing and advertising, the brand is aiming to out maneuver both their direct and indirect competition – while the competition is aiming to out-maneuver the brand. And it's the total combination that produces the results. It's the marketer's job, along with the agency, to look at the results and figure out the reason.

Let's talk about how advertisers out-maneuver the competition in the next chapter.

---

[43] Reeves, Rosser. (2015) *Reality in Advertising*. Widener Classics.
[44] On a similar note, Bill Bernbach is credited with saying, "Nothing kills a bad brand faster than good advertising."

STRATEGIC DEVELOPMENT: READY, AIM, INSIGHTS, & FIRE (THIRD 10 MINUTES)

Ever have one of those friends who says he or she has a great idea for a television commercial? It happens all of the time. One of the reasons most ideas probably wouldn't work is because the concept of the ad is not tied to solving a particular problem.

Yes, there are examples of consumer-generated advertising that have succeeded, but these are few and far between. And, mostly, the problem a brand wanted to solve was consumer engagement – to get more people thinking about and interacting with the brand. Holding an ad contest for people was the way to get it.

On the other hand, **all good professional advertising starts with a strategy**, identifying how the ad will achieve its goals. **What one then does to carry out the strategy is called the tactic**.

In theory, it sounds easy: identify the brand attributes, audience, and situation and you'll find the problem. In other words, develop your strategy for solving the problem, then implement tactics that fall from the strategy.

Done.

Making it even easier, there are only a few possibilities and just a handful of levers you can push. No problem.

THE FOUR KEY TOOLS OF MARKETING

Marketing broadly encompasses everything one does to bring products, services, or ideas to market. In reality, you only have four key decision areas, known as the 4P's, and the answers – when compared against the answers of the competition – will determine the results.

The four key decision areas:

1. **Product:** Which features and benefits should go into it? How should it be designed? And what materials should be used?
2. **Place**: Where should it be sold? Broad distribution would make it easier to purchase, but could make it seem less exclusive.
3. **Price**: What should be charged? A higher price implies better quality and produces higher profits per item, but a lower price could increase sales volume and overall profit.
4. **Promotion**: How should we inform the public? Options include direct selling, public relations, sales promotions (e.g., the use of short-term incentives such as coupons or limited-time games), and, of course, advertising.

Some marketers also include a fifth P – either "packaging" for products and "people" or process for services, while others consider these as part of the product or promotional decisions. Either way, packaging and product labeling play a key role in the perception of the brand and should be included as a key part of the branding and communication decisions.

TO INCREASE THE PRICE, CHANGE THE PACKAGING

The four (or five or six) P's all work in tandem, and you might need to change one when you change another. For instance, since it is hard to compare, a marketer might decide to slightly increase the size of the package when they need to increase the price, with the increase in price being slightly larger than the volume increase. Or they might do the opposite, moving to a slightly smaller package and price and with a slightly less reduction in price. Either bigger or smaller, the cost per ounce would go up.

While pricing and packaging is technically a marketing issue, the ad professional is often called on to make the change seem palatable by finding a benefit to communicate about it. Sometimes the **account executive**, the individual in charge of managing the account at the agency, might suggest this type of strategy to the client when a price change is being discussed to make the agency's job easier than having to explain an obvious price increase.

PRE-EMPTION, USP, & POSITIONING

Remember **pre-emption** from Chapter 1? Rosser Reeves, mentioned in Chapter 2, built on it with the idea of the **Unique Selling Proposition** (USP) – making the "star" of an ad messaging a feature exclusive to the product or service that prospects want. A classic example of this approach was the tagline for M&Ms, "it melts in your mouth, not in your hands."

The problem today is that many now question whether most brands have actual USPs. Competitors in a category are virtually the same, except for the branding. If you can find a clear USP, however, use it. This could be the start of your messaging strategy.

Appearing after USP was established, two marketing consultants, Jack Trout and Al Ries, came up with the idea of **positioning**.[45] Based on the belief that the brain could only hold one idea for a brand in a category – which has been discredited as people actually hold multiple associations about multiple brands and are open to purchasing options beyond their top preference – they allowed four options for ads: leader, the anti, the niche, and the start of a new subcategory.[46]

Today, however, many practitioners just use positioning to describe how their brand compares to the competition in the category for a particular audience.

While often helpful, a problem with many classic marketing approaches is that they're from the marketer's point of view. Successful advertisers put themselves in the shoes of your consumers if you are to connect with them. One advertiser even translated the **4P's** into the **4C's** – customers (what do they need and want), convenience (where do they want to get it), costs (what does it take to get it), and communication (how, when, and in what tone do they want to be reached)?[47] In addition, with social media this communication could also include conversations with the brand (or, at least, what the person monitoring the social media mentions for the brand).

Leo Burnett once said that, "if you can't turn yourself into your customer, you probably shouldn't be in the ad writing business at all."[48] He's right, of course. Seeing through the eyes of the customer is what drives the development of powerful insights into the target audience that form the

---

[45] Ries, Al. & Trout, Jack. (2001) *Positioning: The Battle For Your Mind*. Chicago, McGraw-Hill Education.
[46] Ries, Al. & Trout, Jack. (2001) *Positioning: The Battle For Your Mind*. Chicago, McGraw-Hill Education.
[47] The Marketing Mix. (Nd) *Marketing Mix 4C's*. [Online] Available from: http://marketingmix.co.uk/marketing-mix-4cs/ [Accessed 20 December 2017].
[48] Rieck, Dean. (2005) The Brilliant Words of Leo Burnett. *Direct Creative* . [Online] Available from: http://www.directcreative.com/the-brilliant-words-of-leo-burnett.html [Accessed 30 January 2018].

foundation for creating the products, services, and communications that will ultimately appeal to them.

But while everyone in the advertising and marketing industry should be able to "become the customer," there's one department in the agency world that specializes in it – the **Account Planning** Department.

WELCOME TO ACCOUNT PLANNING

Account planning represents a key link in the strategic process, in that they are tasked with translating the marketing organization's objectives into a focused assignment for the creatives, including vetting relevant information, identifying the opportunity and actionable insights into the target consumer, and developing a strategy for achieving success.

On a broader level, account planners are supposed to be the strategic guardian of the marketing process and represent the voice of the consumer to the agency and client. Since they represent the consumer – while the account executive represents the client – account planners are also supposed to be the agency's "conscience" and speak honestly about the problems and opportunities at hand.

The importance of this role to delivering maximally effective work cannot be overstated. Identifying powerful, unique insights and strategies to guide the creative development is the difference between simply "trying harder" and finding actionable ways to obtain more effective creative work.

Think of opposing football teams; both are trying to score and prevent the other from doing the same. Of course, they both try to recruit the best players, and motivate them to try harder; but the difference between winning and losing often comes down to developing newly effective plays and game plans or by identifying weaknesses or opportunities in the opposition which can be effectively exploited.

A NEWER POSITION WITHIN THE INDUSTRY

While account and media services date back to the beginning of the industry and the creative department dates back more than a hundred years, account planning started in Britain in the early sixties. Two people are credited with its formation – Stephen King at J. Walter Thompson London and **Stanley Pollitt,** co-founder of Boase Massimi Pollitt or (BMP), which is now DDB London.

Both separately identified the need for the new discipline around the same time, but for different reasons. So right off the bat, there were two different visions for account planning.

According to Merry Baskin in her article "What Is Account Planning and What Do Account Planners Do Exactly?",[49] King was "dissatisfied with the workings of both the media and marketing departments within his agency," so he "developed a new system of working (the T-Plan or Target Plan) which concentrated on combining consumer research and insights to create more effective, creative advertising."

The resulting document – or brief – not only identified the overall marketing objective, target audience, and creative strategy, among other categories, it also identified the desired consumer response, namely the affective outcome (how you want people to feel about the brand), the cognitive outcome (what you want people to think about the brand), and the conative outcome (what you want people to do after encountering the ad).

Even though King came up with this new system, it's important to note that as one of the first agencies – if not the first – to hire psychologists for insight development, J. Walter Thompson already had a series of **insight**

---

[49] APG. (2001) *What is Account Planning? (and what do Account Planners do exactly?).* [Online] Available from: http://www.apg.org.uk/single-post/2001/04/02/What-is-Account-Planning-and-what-do-account-planners-do-exactly [Accessed 20 December 2017].

questions employees had to answer before starting an ad. Called the Thompson T-Square, these questions were instituted back in 1912.[50] They were:

- What are we selling?
- To whom are we selling?
- Where are we selling?
- When are we selling?
- How are we selling?[51]

In many ways, King's approach just added more nuance to these questions.

Meanwhile, Pollitt was concerned that account executives were "cherry-picking data and key research findings"[52] because they didn't want to challenge the client and, thus, jeopardize the account.

Both Pollitt and King understood the critical importance of sorting and selecting data to improve the results. But while King decided that there should be a new system to address his concerns, Pollitt decided that there should be a new position by partnering a researcher with the account executive.

As Pollitt wrote, the researcher "should be there as a right, with equal status as a working partner. He was charged with ensuring that all the data relevant to key advertising decisions should be properly analyzed, complemented with new research, and brought to bear on judgments of the creative strategy and how the campaign should be appraised."[53]

---

[50] J. Walter Thompson's History of Advertising, https://www.jwt.com/history/ [Accessed June 5, 2018].

[51] Applegate, Edd (2012) *The Rise of Advertising in the United States: A History of Innovation to 1960*, Lanham, MD, Scarecrow Press.

[52] Pollitt, Stanley. (1979) How I Started Account Planning in Agencies. *Campaign*. [20th April 1979] [Online] Available from: http://www.planningaboveandbeyond.com/wp-content/uploads/How-I-started-account-planning-Stanley-Pollitt.pdf [Accessed 24 December 2017].

[53] Pollitt, Stanley. (1979) How I Started Account Planning in Agencies. *Campaign*. [20th April 1979] [Online] Available from: http://www.planningaboveandbeyond.com/wp-

ACCOUNT PLANNING SIXTY YEARS LATER

Even today, how the account planning position is defined, the roles account planners play within their respective employers, and the resulting value they add varies between agencies, including between office to office in some agency networks.

I have heard the account planner's role described this way: if the account executive "owns" the client (and represents their views in the agency), the creative team owns the work (and are emotionally enmeshed with it), and the media department owns the ad placement, then the account planner owns the consumer. In other words, as Brett Robbs & Deborah Morrison wrote in their book, *Idea Industry: How to Crack the Advertising Career Code*, "the planner's job is to ensure that insights are more than personal and idiosyncratic and that they connect with the brand in a way that will drive the client's business."[54] Or as Steel described it, "The planner's role was basically to embrace consumers as partners in the process of developing advertising, to use their input at every stage of the process to inform and sometimes even inspire creative ideas, and to guide and validate the resulting advertising campaign."[55]

---

content/uploads/How-I-started-account-planning-Stanley-Pollitt.pdf [Accessed 24 December 2017].

[54] Robbs, Brett. & Morrison, Deborah. (2008) *Idea Industry: How to Crack the Advertising Career Code*. New York, One Club for Art & Copy.

[55] Steel, Jon. (1998) *Truth, Lies, and Advertising: The Art of Account Planning*. Hoboken, NJ, John Wiley & Sons.

SOME INSIGHTS ON GENERATING INSIGHTS

To uncover insights, the first thing to do is to review all available **secondary research** – studies and data produced by others. Many of these are free and can be found online while others require a payment or are provided as a subscription service. Some include an analysis while others just provide the raw data. It's best to review as much as possible before taking the next step – **primary research**.

With primary research – research the brand generates – the client can get much more customized information related to the problem and brand, but, of course, it costs more.

When conducting research, there are two forms: **qualitative** and **quantitative**. With qualitative, the sample size tends to be smaller and the data is collected through observations (typically of the prospect or consumer in a natural setting or interacting with the product in a lab), one-on-one interviews with the prospect or user, or in a focus group setting, where the prospects or consumers are interviewed by a moderator.

With quantitative, sample sizes are larger than those for qualitative research and should be statistically significant. The data is typically collected through surveys, either online or off. (Of course, one other place to gather quantitative data is through online search trends.) It is usually better to conduct the qualitative study first, which is directional, and then confirm the findings through the larger quantitative study.

Of course, during and after the initial primary research stage, ideas and executions can – and should – be tested. Often this is done by creating alternate versions of the ad – the change needs to be slight – and seeing which one generated the best results.

BRIEFS SHOULD BE BRIEF

The results of the account planner's work – or the account executive, if the agency does not have a planner – should boil down to what is called "a brief," which I first mentioned in chapter 2. A good brief should start with the basics. Depending on the situation, common briefing points include:

- **Target Audience**: An overview of who'll be viewing the advertising, including their current belief or behavior and any key insights the art director and copywriter can use.
- **The Objective**: The goal of the communication (or campaign) and the desired perception of the brand after encountering the advertising and/or the desired behavior change in the audience.
- **The Promise**: An overview of the product and brand, including the benefit or USP.
- **The Reason Why**: The "proof points" as to why one should believe the advertising claim.
- **The Medium:** A description of the place where the ad will go so the creative team has an understanding of the context in which the message will appear.
- **Brand and Legal Mandatories**: The brand colors, fonts, tagline, and stuff that will keep the brand out of trouble.

It is important to note that while William Rosen (CEO of VSA Partners) and I offer a more sophisticated brief and briefing system in our book *The Activation Imperative: How to Build Brands and Business by Inspiring Action*, the basic criteria above are the minimum you need to get started. But once you are on your way or work with bigger, more sophisticated brands, you will want the more sophisticated briefing system.

The briefing process might run counter to your belief that the more freedom a creative person has – or in the case of advertising, the creative team – the better the results. But ask any leading advertising art director or copywriter and they will tell you that the clearer and tighter the brief, the better the work (and more effective, too).

While the client might have lots to say about the product, brand, and its positioning against its competitors, the supporting points should be boiled down to a page. Otherwise, the brief will become unusable for the copywriter and art director. And if the creative team – the copywriter and art director – finds that it contains too much information for it to be useable, or is confusing, they should send it back for editing and clarification. Meanwhile, if the client has a lot background information and/or other key facts they think is important, it should be dropped into a separate document that can go along with the brief.

FUTURE READING: THE FIELDS THAT CONTRIBUTE TO ADVERTISING INSIGHTS

Academically, advertising is studied from many different angles: Psychology, sociology, cultural studies, behavioral economics, and media studies to name a few.

Likewise, people who practice advertising need to understand these disciplines as well, at least on a basic level, because they are the building blocks of developing powerful advertising strategies.

If you end up creating the ad message, however, then additional disciplines come into play: journalism, fiction writing, play writing, poetry, mythology, rhetoric, and more for copywriters. And for art directors, they should study graphic design, typography, visual rhetoric, photography, and film, among other areas.

LET'S GET CREATIVE: COPY, ART DIRECTION, & PRODUCTION (FOURTH 10 MINUTES)

Love it, hate it, or ignore it, the actual ad is the only true "product" of the advertising industry.

While research reports that strategy presentations can be called "products" too, they are only for internal use, rarely ever seen by the public, and are developed as a way to deliver a service – the recommendations – and sell the ad, so that it will run.

In other words, everything is riding on the ad.

And the place where ads are created is the creative department and the three main positions within it are the **creative director**, **art director**, and **copywriter.** Let's meet these individuals.

A MARRIAGE COUNSELOR FOR CREATIVES

The creative director (CD) is the department's leader and sets the work's direction and tone. But be wary when you hear the title. Many "creative directors," in fact, are just working art directors or copywriters – it's easier to give a fancier title than a bigger salary.

In many ways, the actual CD works as a marriage counselor, enabling art directors and copywriters to work productively together. CDs match them up and help them get unstuck, work through conflicts, and produce better work.

The art director and copywriter work as a team to develop the campaign's "big idea" and the individual elements within it. Within a team, the copywriter is responsible for the words: the ad's headline and body copy; television or radio spot's dialogue and voiceover; and theme or tag line. Copywriters occasionally will come up with the visual idea as well.

Meanwhile, art directors are responsible for an advertisement's visual aspects, including the pictures or images, font choices (when not dictated in brand guidelines), and layouts, and oversee production of the element to ensure overall design fitness. Just as often as copywriters coming up with visual ideas, art directors write the headlines and copy.

Often, the team works so closely together, they can't even say who came up with what and, even if they could, it was the result of their back and forth discussions (and perhaps some arguments) that got them there.

Bigger creative departments might also employ **graphic designers,** who work with the art directors to tighten layouts, clean up images, polish the kerning (i.e., the spacing of the lettering on an ad), and oversee other aspects of ad production to ensure utmost design fitness. In some agencies, they participate in the brainstorming to bring design thinking, a more systems-oriented approach, to the solution.

"With pure design, you almost exclusively use implicit communication to give people a feeling or elicit a mood...with art direction, you want to communicate something specific, so you use different amounts and kinds of design," says ad legend Alex Bogusky,[56] a graphic designer by training.

In some agencies, there's also a **traffic** or **project management** department, who help shepherd the elements through the development

---

[56] Minsky, Laurence (2007) *How to Succeed in Advertising When All You Have Is Talent.* Chicago, The Copy Workshop.

process, ensuring delivery within budget and deadlines. Finally, many larger agencies also have **art buyers**, who negotiate with photographers, illustrators, stock houses, and other suppliers; some have **production** departments that can shoot and edit photography and video.

THE ELEMENTS OF AN AD MESSAGE

Within the messaging that copywriters and art directors are creating, there are five main elements: The **headline, visual, body copy, tagline,** and **logo**. For long copy communications and some short ones, there are also **subheads**, smaller **inset imagery**, and/or **captions** under selected imagery. Some also might have **legal** copy at the bottom or, in the case of a pharmaceutical ad, on the following page.

Thinking about the role of the **headline** and **visual** is sort of like thinking about the chicken and the egg. In some instances, the headline comes first and in others, the visual takes priority. Whichever leads, its job is to capture attention. The one that follows then reframes the attention-grabbing element. It might advance your initial stopping message – or make the reader re-think it. The combination conveys the main message.

As ad legend **Bruce Bendinger** defines it, a headline is the initial verbal connection to the ad and the main image is the initial visual connection.[57]

The **copy then helps tell the story**. It can be just a few words in some ads and long and detailed in others. It can be written like a news story (with the most important information at the top going down to the least), short story, poem, first-person testimonial, or use some other rhetorical

---

[57] Bendinger, Bruce et al (2009) *The Copy Workshop Workbook 4th Edition*, Chicago, IL: The Copy Workshop.

device. It can have some attitude, based on the idea and the brand personality.

Next, **the logo identifies the brand**. It should not be touched or changed. The logo helps bring brand consistency from one piece of communication to another.

Finally, a **tagline** (or theme line; also, called a strap line if you're in England) sums up the campaign or message, the campaign's key idea. Everything else should track back to it, helping communicate the brand promise.

Taglines rarely work as headlines. They're not the same. Famous taglines include: "Just Do It" by Nike and "I'm Lovin' It" by McDonald's.

The rule of thumb when developing advertising is if you can remove an element or more and can still convey the meaning, then you should remove it. However, be cautious. Most beginners tend to under communicate, resulting in an ad that is confusing.

THE HIERARCHY OF YOUR MESSAGE

Once you have the elements of your ad, the idea is to drive people through it. Good art directors ask, "what do we want them to read or see first, second, third, and so on until all of the needed parts have been consumed?"

They then design the ad in the order the elements are meant to be seen. Think of a stand-up comedian telling a joke: there's a set-up and a punch-line. This is a good way to remember the interaction between the headline and the key visual. But which one serves as the attention grabber and which one provides the payoff depends on the concept.

Rarely, if ever, does one want the body copy to be read before the headline and visual are consumed. Generally, copy becomes more interesting and effective after the interplay between the key visual and headline (or is it headline and key visual?).

The logo should only be placed so it's seen first if the goal is to reinforce the current brand image. If the goal is to change perceptions or announce news – the bulk of most advertising – the logo should come at the end as the sign off.

Finally, once the hierarchy of elements has been determined, art directors play with the placement and size of the various parts to emphasize the importance of each.

SOAK UP IDEAS & WRITE THEM DOWN

As for coming up with an ad idea or concept, you might want to first keep a record of interesting images and ideas: "If I'm watching a movie and I see something funny or I see something on the street, I sort of file it away. It's like a novelist who overhears a conversation and jots it down," says Ted Bell, former vice chairman of Y&R, who went on to become a highly successful novelist. "[The novelist] doesn't know what he's going to use it for, but somewhere down the line you'll see that conversation in a book. You'd be surprised at how many famous advertising ideas first saw the light of day on a cocktail napkin."[58]

---

[58] Minsky, Laurence (2007) *How to Succeed in Advertising When All You Have Is Talent*. Chicago, The Copy Workshop.

ADVERTISING SHOULDN'T SOUND LIKE ADVERTISING

While we're talking about creating paid marketing messages – and some owned ones – you don't want it to sound like "advertising."

Rather, you want it to sound like your brand's personality – empathetic, approachable, natural, friendly, or whatever it claims in the brand guide. In other words, good ad copy should sound conversational, like you're talking to your neighbor over a fence or to your buddy at the bar. It's cool to use slang. Have fragments.

And, start sentences – even paragraphs – with "and." Because that's how people talk.

It should never sound stiff nor formal, unless, of course, that's the brand's image or it's part of the idea you're dramatizing.

To get to a good headline, copywriters will often write hundreds of them, then go back and find the good one. The same goes for writing the body copy – i.e., the support copy following the headlines and subheads. David Ogilvy once wrote, "I am a lousy copywriter, but I am a good editor. So, I go to work editing my own draft. After four or five editings, it looks good enough to show to the client."[59]

In the end, make sure the ad isn't boring or it could become wallpaper. It's been estimated that people are exposed to approximately 10,000 brand messages a day.[60] If it doesn't stand out through surprise, emotion, entertainment, or something else, your message will get lost.

---

[59] Ogilvy, David. (1986) *The Unpublished David Ogilvy: A Selection of His Writings from the Files of His Partners*. New York, Ogilvy Group.

[60] Saxon, Joshua. (2017) Why Your Customers' Attention is the Scarcest Resource in 2017. *American Marketing Association*. [Online] Available from: https://www.ama.org/partners/content/Pages/why-customers-attention-scarcest-resources-2017.aspx [Accessed 19 December 2017].

TELL YOUR STORY

I often have beginning advertising students find the common storylines, language, and imagery of a category and create their ads to fit right into it. This makes their work sound like "advertising," an easy strategy to break, and most eventually do.

To get beyond the feeling of advertising, you can start by telling your story and how the product helped solve a problem in your life, based from your perspective. After all, what makes you unique will make your work unique too. Then you can expand and write other stories based on the descriptions of the prospects in the brief and your research.

Working on a diverse team also helps. My friend Steven Cartozian called it "creating a genius," because everyone on the team contributes their strengths and unique perspectives and, when done right, eliminates their weakness.

The agency that broke the old formula and brought creative messaging to the forefront is Doyle Dane Bernbach (DDB), the place responsible for advertising's creative revolution in the 1960s. Before DDB, mainstream advertising was primarily staid, insular, boring.

The visionary who led DDB was Bill Bernbach. As mentioned in chapter 2, while he got the idea from Paul Rand, he started pairing copywriters with art directors to develop ideas, where previously a writer developed the copy and then handed it to an art director to produce. Bernbach was fed up with the direction of the industry, which was more focused on technique than on the art of persuasion.

Now, starting with DDB, **the emphasis was on the idea**.

Bill Bernbach did something else, too. He hired people from then marginalized groups – people who were not generally represented in mainstream ad agencies of the day including those of Jewish, Irish, Italian, and Greek descent – who brought their stories, imagery, and sensibilities to general marketing, making the advertising better and fresher in the process.[61]

African Americans also began breaking into general advertising, an easy increase since there were only two working in a general advertising agency in New York in the 1950s.[62] And, while there was a longer track record of women in mainstream advertising, – dating back to 1908 when Helen Lansdowne Resor joined what was to become J. Walter Thompson – more women started entering the field during this time.

Today, however, true diversity is still lacking. For instance, only 11% of creative directors are female.[63] And based on data from 2008 – the most recent figures I could find – only 5.8% of agency employees and 3.2% of agency executives and managers are African-American.[64]

Not only is this wrong from an ethical standpoint, it also continues to negatively impact the quality of work produced by the industry. To "create the genius" mentioned above, the industry needs people with diverse histories, perspectives, insights, experiences, and abilities. On another note, increased diversity helps keep the agency from making unintentional errors, which is why major advertisers are now pressuring shops to diversify their staffing.[65]

---

[61] Bernbach, Willam. (2003) AdWeek . [Online] Available from: http://adage.com/article/adage-encyclopedia/bernbach-william/98346/ [Accessed 30 January 2018].

[62] Black Americans in Advertising Timeline 1940s-1960s. (2017) *Bold Culture by Streamlined*. [Online] Available from: http://boldculture.co/black-americans-advertising-timeline-1940s-1950s/ [Accessed 24 December 2017].

[63] Cohen, David. (2017) Only 11 Percent of Creative Directors are Women and Pinterest Wants to Right the Ratio. *AdWeek*. [Online] Available from:
http://www.adweek.com/digital/pinterest-right-the-ratio/ [Accessed 30 January 2018].

[64] Wheaton, Ken. (2008) Top Lawyer Preps March on Mad Avenue, AD Age [Online] Available from: http://adage.com/article/agency-news/top-lawyer-preps-march-mad-ave/130968/ [Accessed 26, 2018].

[65] Mallia, K. L. & Windels, K. (2018) "Female Representation among Advertising's Creative Elite: A Content Analysis of the *Communication Arts Advertising Annual*." *Advertising & Society Quarterly*, vol. 18 no. 4, 2018. Project MUSE, [Online] Available from: muse.jhu.edu/article/684250. [Accessed: 26, January 2018].

SOME KEY CONSIDERATIONS WHEN CREATING ADVERTISING

When developing an ad, the copywriter and art director need to settle on an executional format or framework. Options include: product demonstrations; realistic or fantasy story; user, celebrity, or authority endorsement; comparisons; problem-and-solution; parody; and more.

The team also needs to determine tonality: should they use humor or incite fear? should they be direct or speak in metaphors? should they be snarky or come across as sophisticated?

I can continue, but you get the idea – every aspect needs to be thought through.

Informing and guiding the team's thinking is, of course, the brief, particularly the goal of what the prospects should think, feel, and do after encountering the ad message. Once the concepts have been created, the team needs to show how the resulting message answers the brief and solves the problem.

SEE & SAY IS NOT THE SOUTION

One more thing: if you see it in the visual, you don't need to say it. And, conversely, if you say it in the headline, you don't need to see it.

The best ads work when the visual implies one thing and the headline implies another and when brought together in the brain of the consumer, a third meaning is constructed. This is the classic DDB structure that helped bring the creative advertising revolution.

Some call this stronger approach the 1 + 1 = 3 formula, because, when combined, the visual and headline is greater than the sum of its parts.[66]

Yes, you can find many see-and-say ads – clients seem to like them – but examples that actually got noticed and remembered are very rare. My suggestion is to use the see-and-say construction cautiously and, rather, focus on using the 1 + 1 = 3 formula. As ad legend Howard Gossage once said, "When you design a mousetrap, be sure to leave room for the mouse."[67] See-and-say doesn't.

BE OPEN TO BREAKING THE RULES

Back when I was a student in college, I took a poetry-writing course that turned out to be a big influence on my writing career hawking hamburgers, pickles, and other consumer and business-to-business goods.

Early in the trimester, the professor said that there are many words that inherently sound "poetic" and that we were, henceforth, banned from using them. He believed that these words were a cheap way to create false emotion and had been used to death by those trying to sound lyrical.

Now I bet you're about to say that I followed his advice, which is half correct. Most of the time, I tried to be as simple with my language as possible. And I found that it worked.

But in the course, I set out to write a poem that incorporated all of the banned words. It was fun to write, self-referential, filled with self-

---

[66] Minsky, Laurence. (2007) How to Succeed in Advertising When All You Have Is Talent. Chicago, The Copy Workshop.
[67] Gossage, Howard. (2017) *Ad Teachings*. [Online] Available from: http://www.adteachings.com/post/107111911040/heres-a-useful-quote-from-the-legendary [Accessed 27 December 2017].

awareness, irony and humor, and was a break from the woe-is-me, overly sensitive poetry the class had been producing.

My professor loved it.

I bring this up because I suggested you stay away from expected structures, language, and images.

But at times, you can use them. Like the poem I wrote that incorporated all of the banned words, a student occasionally challenges my advice, picks an overused structure or approach, and, using fresh, self-aware, self-referential, ironic language, produces a unique, never-seen-before campaign.

I think that's great. I wish I could see more advertising that's fresh, surprising, reinvented. I bet you do too, because it's what gets people to stop, smile, remember, and talk about your ad.

So, here's my challenge. If you're creating advertising, explore how you can reinvent old conventions while inventing new ones. Or if you're a client reviewing the advertising, reward surprise and freshness. And if you're not in the industry, you now know why most advertising falls short.

But there might be one more reason your ad falls short. It's the ad placement – a topic we'll cover in the next chapter.

YOUR TRUE MESSAGE: MEDIA CHOICES & MEDIA CHANNELS (FIFTH 10 MINUTES)

Pioneering media studies professor **Marshall McLuhan** wrote that the medium is the message. (Actually, the title of his classic book is *The Medium is the Massage*, because of a typesetting error, which McLuhan decided to keep because he thought the word was more appropriate.)[68]

One of the pioneers of **media studies**, McLuhan argued that a new medium actually changes culture, perhaps even more so than the content that resides in it. For a near current example, McLuhan, who passed away in 1980 – twenty-seven years before the premier of the iPhone – would have pointed out that mobile devices changed society more than the apps that appear on them.

And he was right. On a macro-level, Snapchat, Maps, Words with Friends, and all of the other mobile applications have changed society far less than the mere fact of the existence of mobile and its ability to find anything and everything you want "right here" and "right now."

---

[68] Commonly Asked Questions (And Answers). (2017) *Marshall McLuhan*. [Online] Available from: https://www.marshallmcluhan.com/common-questions/ [Accessed 24 December 2017].

Because of the immediacy of mobile, marketing had to change, and the way advertisers talked to consumers, particularly on that platform, had to be different as well.

THE CONTEXT IS THE MESSAGE, TOO

Beyond the culture-shaping force of a new medium, the advertising context matters too, even in long-existing mediums. Ads mostly live in someone else's "house," be it a website, blog, vlog, TV show (broadcast or streaming), radio program (terrestrial or internet), social media site, or elsewhere. Even outdoor billboards reside in the broader context of the highway, street, or downtown "pedway" where they're posted. And, for shopping, the packaging and other brand messaging will be seen in the context of the store environment that is "hosting" it.

The choice of media placement telescopes meaning about the brand being advertised. Running your ad on Fox *implies* one set of brand values while advertising on MSNBC another. Advertisers can get themselves into trouble when their ad appears in a vehicle that promotes ideas and imagery at odds with the values and personality they want their brand to represent.

Meanwhile, the ability to stand out within a media placement is key. For instance, if you're a car manufacturer, too many other car ads in a general publication might make it hard to get noticed. The exception: specialty venues. Since car enthusiasts read blogs and magazines, visit websites, and watch shows dedicated to cars, placing your car ad in one of these environments might make sense, depending on your message and ability to stand out.

MEDIA BOUGHT & SOLD

As mentioned earlier, your first need is to get the right message at the right place at the right time to achieve your objective.

Figuring out the right message was the subject of the previous chapter. Figuring out how to be in the "right place at the right time" is the mission of the media professionals, who fall into one of two groups. On the agency or client side, there are **media planners** and buyers who identify the optimal media channels and then purchase the time and space.

To identify and select the channel, the planners and buyers first look to see if it delivers to the audience the marketer is trying to reach. They then look at the other adverts on the outlet to ensure that their client can stand out. Another consideration: the quality of the outlet to elevate the impression of a brand, called a "**halo effect**." Finally, they look at the costs: what does it take to run the ad, based on the "**CPM**," which means the **cost per thousand** people reached through the placement.

And on the "publishing" side, there are media salespeople who, like others in sales, are pushing their product. While they are a great source of tickets to play-off games, sold out concerts, and other exclusive events that you could use entertaining clients (or yourself), they're also a great source for audience information to help you decide if their outlet is right for your brand, if there are other advertising options you can use, and the potential timing and media schedule. And, of course, they conduct any price negotiations for the placement.

If you are launching a new brand that is directly competing against another brand that is advertising on a certain website, the visitor-ship information for it can give you insights into your intended audience, including age and income – and could result in identifying other places where you might want to advertise.

Call it the poor brand's form of market research. One caveat, however: The brand that is advertising on the website might have made a poor choice and selected the wrong site, but it is still a good place to start, even for brands with larger advertising budgets.

DEVELOPING THE PLAN

The first step for the media planner or buyer is to either determine or confirm the goals for the campaign.

While media is following creative development in this book, the plan can be and often is developed before the messaging is developed – and the media plan would obviously need to be determined before the individual messaging elements are created. (It's another chicken-and-egg situation, because an ad concept might lead to the placement strategy, just as a media placement opportunity can lead to a concept.)

Media planners can then work either one of two ways to achieve those goals: 1) build a plan based on the goals to determine the budget or 2) start with the budget and see how far they can go in reaching the goal. Unless one has an unlimited budget, it's often the second route or a paring back of the first one that ends up being the final plan.

One of the key questions the media planners needs to answer, particularly when working within a budget, is should the brand aim for "**reach**" and try to talk to more prospects or aim for "**frequency**" and increase the number of times a single prospect encounters the message? The answer will help determine how often the campaign needs to run across all media channels.

In an ideal world with an unlimited budget, except for seasonal products or services, the ad campaign would run continuously. And some brands do employ that media schedule. Other brands might run continuously and then increase the amount at selected intervals. Another option is go the opposite direction and have heavy periods of running the advertising with other times going completely quiet, which is called "**flighting**" or have equal amounts of running the campaign and quiet, which is called "**blinkering**."[69]

Media planners also compare the strengths and weaknesses of each medium against the stated objectives to find the optimal mix across channels. Some media "interrupts" the audience with an ad and others work when people go to the ad. Likewise, some offer more of a one-way communication and are essentially counting "eyeballs" or the number of people exposed to it, while others count interactions and conversations, which looks at how many people engage with the message, react to it, forward it, talk back to the marketer through social media messaging, and purchase the product or service. Often, media planners want a combination of the two.

OPTIONS, OPTIONS, OPTIONS

While my book, *The Activation Imperative*, co-written with William Rosen, provides details on the best practices of each media discipline, here are some brief strengths and weaknesses:

- **TV**: The most "Hollywood" of options. Sound. Motion. The ability to dramatize a product, create interest, and build the brand to a large audience. But the cost tends to be hefty and production tends to take longer.
- **Pre-Roll**: Since the spots in front of YouTube and other online videos often give viewers the ability to skip them after six seconds, pre-roll may need to be constructed differently than broadcast TV, but it has many of its same pluses and minuses.

---

[69] Bendinger, Bruce. (2009) *Advertising and the Business of Brands*. Chicago, The Copy Workshop.

- **General Interest Magazines**: You can take it anywhere, has lots of pass-along value – think of the doctor's office – and you can convey detailed, complex ideas and information. Plus, you have strong brand-building capabilities. But production lead times are long, it can often be cluttered, and overall print readership is declining.
- **Special Interest Magazines**: By their nature, they can deliver a highly-interested audience. But they tend to be even more cluttered than general interest publications.
- **Newspapers**: Though readership is plummeting, the people still reading them are looking for news and seeking information, thus making newspapers a good place to announce a sale. Lead times are also relatively short. Print quality, however, can be low and the environment can be cluttered, so it can be hard to stand out.
- **Radio:** Highly local and efficient, you'll reach people while they're on the go and perhaps ready to buy. As a result, radio is a good place to remind people about your brand. When creating a radio ad, you need to keep in mind that your audience must catch the message right away, because it goes away; it is in a highly-cluttered environment, and listeners are quick to change channels when commercials start. (Although I don't recall the source, I heard it said that call-in shows and eyewitness reports were the original social media.)
- **Internet Radio & Podcasts**: Radio is going through a reinvention with the rise of Internet radio and advent of podcasts.[70] With the benefit of displaying a visual on the device (mobile, laptop, desktop) and the power to click to a website, Internet radio gives advertisers the power of interactivity and immediacy. But audiences are still small.
- **Outdoor**: Since people often take the same route for their daily commute, you can ensure message frequency. But people can also tune it out because they see the same one so often and the environment is typically cluttered. Finally, the message must be very short. Powerful for getting people to stop, but not for changing one's perception of a product.
- **Experiential:** Events and other activities offer high engagement, but reach is small, and costs can be high. They work best when attendees can post on social media, enabling the advertiser to extend their reach through these updates. It can also work well for business-to-business

---

[70] Rosen, William. & Minsky, Laurence. (2017) *The Activation Imperative: How to Build Brands and Business by Inspiring Action*. Lanham, MD, Rowman & Littlefield.

audiences, where the number of prospects is small, and each sale is typically larger than those for consumer products.
- **Online Banners**: While it lets you get the message to the appropriate people and build **brand awareness**, banners are often in cluttered environments and could be in places where the content is at odds with the brand's values. Finally, the click-through rate is often low.
- **Direct Mail**: Research indicates that nearly 100% of it gets seen by the recipient,[71] which makes sense because people have to determine if it's a bill or another important notice before discarding. And they're good for including response mechanisms such as coupons, so you'll know if they work. But people often find them annoying – not good for brand building – and they are often very expensive when compared against other options.
- **PPC (Pay Per Click):** Since you only pay when someone clicks on your ad and you can turn it on and off very quickly, you can control your budget and know the effectiveness of your messages, a way to test them before running in more expensive places with longer lead times. Plus, it reaches the very people who are actively researching your product's category on Google and other Internet search engines. But it doesn't give you the opportunity to build the brand image or convey much information.
- **Social**: Posting on Facebook, LinkedIn, Pinterest, Twitter, Instagram, and other platforms are strong ways to show you understand prospects, reinforce the brand with customers, and create awareness with others. And you can respond quickly to any negative comments. But managing it could be very time intensive, something few realize before they get started with it.
- **Mobile**: It can be a powerful tool for providing information to people who need or desire it immediately. And because it's often the last medium viewed before making a purchase and people spend lots of time on it, mobile can be – and often is – the key to marketing success. But it's typically not as effective as a brand-building tool.
- **E-mail:** You control the environment, the cost is low, and it could be effective for re-marketing, the goal of re-engaging a previous prospect or

---

[71] 3 Tips to Make Your Direct Mail Stand Out. (2015) *D Brief*. [Online] Available from: http://www.dmediaweb.com/1889/direct-mail-tips-to-stand-out/ [Accessed 27 December 2017].

- customer. But when was the last time you reviewed all of the emails in your junk filter? Enough said.
- **In-Store**: Shopping – and particularly at the shelf where shoppers can either select your brand or the competitor's is your "moment of truth."[72] Messaging can sway that decision, but creating it requires long lead times and getting it displayed often relies on the willingness of the retailer and the work of their employees or suppliers, which could be expensive.

The list can continue, and placement opportunities are only limited by creativity and the willingness of potential partners. Stickers or printing on fresh fruit at the market, for example, could be a creative option for blender manufacturers or yogurt purveyors.

WHAT MORE CAN YOU GET?

One thing media buyers explore when negotiating with media outlets is potential add-ons. For instance, with radio, a brand might be able to get a banner ad on their website and co-sponsorships of events.

The goal with your plan is to align the media buy to get more out of the investment. For instance, if they know prospects commute to work in a car, tend to listen to country stations, and make their dinner solutions on the way home from work, then a combination of radio and outdoor might make the most sense. On the other hand, if the prospect is someone who plans ahead, then TV advertising the night before might work best.

---

[72] Hollis, Nigel. (2006) Making the Most of the Moment of Truth. *Millward Brown's POV*. [Online] Available from: http://www.millwardbrown.com/docs/default-source/insight-documents/points-of-view/MillwardBr own_POV_MomentOfTruth.pdf [Accessed 30 JAnuary 2018].

More sophisticated media planning involves studying the customer journey to identify the key points on the prospect's path-to-purchase. Once they know the path, they can identify the advertising platforms that would be most effective at each point along the path.[73]

PROGRAMMATIC CAN BE PROBLEMATIC

Meanwhile, a newer type of online media buying, programmatic, can help relieve some of the labor intensiveness for mobile, social, and other digital formats, because the purchasing is being conducted by algorithms developed through **artificial intelligence** based on the predicted or observed behaviors of your prospects.

In addition, the brand can then ensure that their digital ads follow people once they visit their website, through a media-buying strategy called "**re-targeting**," where a "cookie" is planted on the visitor's computer to enable ads to show up on other websites that reinforce the message.

Context, however, is one key problem associated with algorithmic purchasing. While your prospect may enjoy certain sites – or types of sites – the brand might not want to be associated with them. As the use of artificial intelligences improves, however, this issue might become less prevalent.[74]

---

[73] More can be found on the use of journey maps in my book with William Rosen, "The Activation Imperative" – Rosen, William. & Minsky, Laurence. (2017) *The Activation Imperative: How to Build Brands and Business by Inspiring Action*. Lanham, MD, Rowman & Littlefield.

[74] Vranica, Suzanne. (2017) Advertisers Try to Avoid the Web's Dark Side from Fake News to Extremist Videos. *The Wall Street Journal*. [Online] Available from: https://www.wsj.com/articles/advertisers-try-to-avoid-the-webs-dark-side-from-fake-news-to-extremist-videos-1497778201 [Accessed 27 December 2017].

Another issue is online fraud. With PPC, programmatic buying, and occasionally manual purchasing – the "eyeballs" the invoice says the brand is reaching might not actually be humans, but, rather, robots, hitting on the ad links.[75] Industry trade associations such as the Association of National Advertisers (ANA) are working on addressing this issue.[76] But, in the meantime, be wary of audience claims.

Finally, tracking consumers through the use of cookies and re-targeting them with follow-up ads can lead to all sorts of ethical questions and issues, particularly around consumer rights to privacy. In the European Union, with its **General Date Protection Regulation (GDPR),** it can lead to legal issues as well for advertisers who serve European citizens, even if the business is located in the US.[77]

BACK TO ADVERTISING'S ROOTS

Recall, media buying-and-selling is how the modern advertising industry started. It almost feels like we are traveling in a full circle. And in many ways, we have.

---

[75] Smith, Kevin. (2015) Robots Just Stole Half Your Programmatic Media Buy. *Creative Intelligence*. [Online] Available from: http://blog.iqagency.com/robots-stole-half-programmatic-media-buy/ [Accessed 27 December 2017].

[76] Smith, Kevin. (2015) Robots Just Stole Half Your Programmatic Media Buy. *Creative Intelligence*. [Online] Available from: http://blog.iqagency.com/robots-stole-half-programmatic-media-buy/ [Accessed 27 December 2017].

[77] Minsky, Laurence & Quesenberry, Keith A. (2018) Hunter or Hunted? How Digital Media and GDPR Increases Importance of Inbound B2B Sales, *European Business Review*, January – February, 55 – 58.

Likewise, running advertising provides a feedback loop. All things being equal, did it make people like your brand more? was the brand able to charge more or earn more over its life? did sales improve? did the brand and the brand's owner enjoy other business benefits after running the campaign?

These are questions you need to ask after running a campaign. Let's touch on post-campaign analysis in the next chapter. Plus, we'll explore other assorted questions and topics about advertising as we reach our destination – a complete book on advertising in under one hour.

ONWARD: ANALYSIS, AGENCY SELECTION, & NEXT STEPS

(FINAL 10 MINUTES)

Within the ad industry, there is a history of media fraud, as mentioned in the previous chapter; and it grew in the 1800s, promoting "snake oil" and other solutions of questionable quality.

But over the years, the industry has worked to improve its image. While Helen Lansdowne Resor, whom we met in Chapter 4, was raising the industry's level of creativity at J. Walter Thompson as the agency's creative director, her husband, Stanley B. Resor, who was part of a group that purchased the agency in 1916 and served as CEO for the next 39 years,[78] was working to raise the industry's level of respect. His efforts included instituting a training program at J. Walter Thompson, hiring a Harvard professor to lead research, demanding that advertising be created based on "scientific" processes and, in 1917, working to help start the Association of American Advertising Agencies (the 4A's), which promoted ethical standards for the industry.[79]

---

[78] Resor, Stanley B. (1879-1962) (2003) AdAge (online) http://adage.com/article/adage-encyclopedia/resor-stanley-b-1879-1962/98851/ [Accessed 6 June 2017].

[79] American Association of Advertising Agencies. (2003) *AdAge*. [Online] Available from: http://adage.com/article/adage-encyclopedia/american-association-advertising-agencies/98313/ [Accessed 24 December 2017].

As a result, there are codes of ethics for promoting sin products and marketing to children and other vulnerable groups; there are laws and regulations to follow; and there is an occasional public outcry when campaigns go wrong.

All help keep advertising in check and all angles should be explored before the campaign is launched.

The key question to ask, after a campaign has started, should be about its effectiveness. Did it work? Did it achieve the objectives? Did sales go up? Did the brand affinity improve? Are more people mentioning the brand without prompting than before the campaign? What did they think of it before the campaign and what do they think of it after? Finally, what is the perception of the brand (i.e., was the brand repositioned?)

The advertiser doesn't have to answer "yes" to all of these questions – just the ones that are related to the original goal of the campaign.

After all, some of the questions might be at odds with others.

For instance, the final question – repositioning – is an important one and might take place without increasing the sales volume or the immediate profits. One use of advertising is to move the brand from one audience to another. Say the first audience is getting older and decreasing. To enable a longer life for the brand, the owner would need to reposition it for younger customers. As a result, the current customers might switch to a different brand, making for an even trade in the short-term. But the firm ensures a longer overall life for the brand.

IT'S A DECISION-MAKING BUSINESS

The more the advertiser learns from their post-campaign analysis, the better they will be at making decisions when developing their next campaign. Beside crafting of the words, images, and sounds in the advertising creative elements, all an individual or ad agency has to sell is the quality of its decision-making abilities. And decision-making on the client side is just as key.

One of the biggest decisions for advertisers is who to use for creating the advertising. Get the wrong one and the advertiser could spend lots of money for very little return – or even hurt the brand.

Meanwhile, agencies need to decide what type of clients they want to attract. Get the wrong clients and they might not be able to get the right ones, because the agency won't have the samples to show. And the opportunity cost of serving the wrong client might be too draining as well.

WHAT SHOULD CLIENTS SEEK IN AN AGENCY?

The first question should be, are they strategic and do they have a track record of creating innovative, effective advertising solutions? Ask the agency leaders how they solved problems for previous clients. Stay away from those that have a habit of repeating the same type of solution for different clients.

Second, does the agency understand the brand and audience? While not a requirement, it helps if they know how to effectively approach similar audiences.

Third, do they work hard? Stopping at the first idea will not generate truly new solutions, so the odds of it being noticed go down.

Fourth, where are they strong and how do they make their money? An ad agency that produces lots of social media posts will be less likely to suggest a TV campaign even if it's the best approach for solving the problem. The job of the advertiser is to understand what media they need to use for the best result and hire the specialist agencies that can help them achieve their goals.

And do you like them? Can the client spend hours in a room with people from the agency? And does the client trust them to the extent that they are willing to bet their house and job on them?

Finally, what does the gut say? That's a strong indicator, too.

A weak indicator is spec work – advertising messaging created during the pitch to impress the potential client. This approach tends to be tactical without the upfront strategy. And it is rarely original or based on true insights about the brand, the audience, and the problem, because the client and their proprietary information is an integral part of identifying the actual problem that needs to be solved.

WHAT DO AGENCIES SEEK IN A CLIENT?

The client/agency relationship also needs to be a match on both sides. In my book, *How to Succeed in Advertising When All You Have Is Talent* (Second Edition), Stan Richards outlined what he seeks in a client and can serve as a good guide here (quoting from the book):

"The first question to ask is can we do great work?" says Richards. "Is the client open to get creative? Do they trust fresh ideas? And are they willing to provide enough input to get it?"

The second question focuses on getting results. "Can we measure how the advertising works or are we going to have to be satisfied that the client's spouse thinks it's nice?" he asks. "It's important to measure results.

Being able to look at sales and determine whether the advertising did the job is important to effective campaigns in the future."

Remuneration is the third question. "Can we make a profit?" asks Richards. "The client has to understand that we both assume the responsibility of helping each other profit in the relationship."

And the final question looks at the personal relationship with a potential client.

"'Can we have fun?' he asks. "That's the human side. Do we like the people? Do they like us? When we show up for a meeting are we going to be treated with respect? Will we enjoy the experience?"[80]

AD AGENCIES: THE PROFIT PART

As Stan indicated, agencies need to make a profit at what they do. There are three main ways to pay an agency: by media billings, hourly rates, and by value.

With media billings, an approach dating back to the industry's founding, an outlet such as a newspaper published its rates, which the client paid to the agency. However, the rate was discounted 15% to the agency, enabling them to keep the difference. In other words, if the ad cost $100 to place (most are more like $250.000 or even twice that amount for a one-time black-and-white ad in a national magazine), the client pays the agency that amount, the agency pays the medium $85 and they keep the remaining $15 to cover all costs and generate a profit. (For out-of-pocket costs, the agency

---

[80] Minsky, Laurence. (2007) *How to Succeed in Advertising When All You Have Is Talent.* Chicago, The Copy Workshop.

would mark up the expenses by 1.1765% when invoicing the client to get to the approximate 15% differential.)

This model worked when most advertising was placed through large media. But since the agency made most of its money through media placement, it overemphasized and recommended media advertising over other opportunities. And it de-emphasized the need for quality ads.

For the hourly rate approach, an agency can have individual rates for different positions and levels of seniority or one "blended" rate taking into account all of the various salaries. Then the client just buys a bucket of hours which the agency works against or is charged by the number of hours it takes to do something – for instance, conduct a research study, write and design an ad, buy the media. You name it.

A third approach, which is now gaining steam, is to base costs around "value" pricing with a project rate.

More like a "retail" model, the agency sets prices for their various marketing activities. The individual prices are based on overhead and other costs, but also on the value the final element could generate in the marketplace. It might only take an hour for the agency to create an ad, but it will be seen by millions of people and support the launch of a new product, which could generate millions for the client. In this case the agency would charge more than they would for an invitation to a small open house that might only generate a small sale.

Project rates or value pricing, however, can protect the client (they'll know what they'll pay) and enables the agency to understand what they'll earn as well.

Determining the project rate is the trick. There are several things to consider: how much is it worth for the client? how much could they afford? how long will it take? how much will it help the agency's portfolio? And if the advertising works, can the agency charge more in the future?

Most agencies use a combination of all three approaches. And the final rates are based on negotiations between the agency and the client. Of course, clients who want better work know that they need to pay more for better people.

ESTIMATING, APPROXIMATELY SPEAKING

When working on an hourly basis, or even with project value pricing, agencies should start by estimating the project to make sure it will be profitable. To start estimating, the agency needs to know as much about the project as possible by asking questions.

For instance, with the creative development of a website, an agency might ask: how many pages? how much copy per page? is it one design template or does each page change?

For radio, they might want to know: do they need just the script? or will the agency be producing the spots at the recording studio? what about casting? how many rounds of revisions will the agency provide?

For transit and newspaper advertising, the agency might ask: how many concepts are needed? Will there be a photo shoot? does the agency need to provide extensive retouching work?

These are just a few of the questions for executing specific elements, but I think you get the picture.

The answers to any of the questions can change the final estimate. And it gets harder to estimate earlier in the development process, especially when the problem isn't defined.

In other words, there is no real set rate.

The best suggestion for an agency (or a freelancer) is to get the answers in detail to all the questions, figure out how long it will take, then double it (to account for all of the things that weren't considered and to cover for the fact that everything seems easier than it is), propose it to the client and see if he/she can afford and then cut back from there.

The other option for agencies is to see if they can uncover what the client is expecting to pay and then try to determine if they can deliver it for that amount, including any out-of-pocket expenses – e.g., stock photos, music beds, you name it.

Finally, for the sake of both parties, make sure that the agency and client get the final agreement, called a statement of work or scope of work (SOW), in writing. If anything changes in the statement of work, the project should be re-estimated.

A LOOK TO THE FUTURE

I would like to close this short book by sharing a quote from Alex Bogusky: "I don't know why there's such self-loathing in the industry, but ever since I've been in advertising, practitioners have been predicting its demise."

I've noticed this too.

Bogusky made this comment when he was recalling a time when people were talking about the end of print as a dominant medium, and I have been noticing it for the last few years as people talk about the end of TV as a primary source for advertising.

Why does this continually happen? Is it because so many advertising practitioners "fell" into the field after the original career goal of being a poet/singer/novelist/painter/actor/movie maker/professional gambler/guitarist didn't pay off? Perhaps they secretly want advertising to fail so they can get on with their true calling in life. Whatever the cause, it is concerning. How can our clients believe in advertising if the practitioners don't?

Especially since we do know that advertising can work.

Not that it works every time.

But imagine a doctor denouncing all medicine because one patient died on the operating table.

A more interesting approach for people in advertising to take is to embrace change but recognize that most existing media probably won't completely go away within our lifetimes; to recognize what advertising can and can't do and set reasonable expectations with clients; and believe that advertising skills will continue to be needed tomorrow, although the how, what, and where of the practice might change.

A LITTLE KNOWLEDGE GOES A SHORT WAY

I hope this little book inspires you to learn more, because I left off key stories about David Ogilvy, Leo Burnett, and other key players and how they shaped the industry. Many of its stories and the lives of some of its practitioners are more interesting than those in *Mad Men*. And the approaches and techniques they developed can help you as an advertising practitioner or as a business owner.

I also did not spend time on another important role that advertising plays, one that Rory Sutherland so eloquently described in his first TED talk (and I urge you to view it) – that advertising creates value in itself.[81]

As a classic example, back in the early 1960s, DDB took an ugly cheap car – the Volkswagen Beetle – and redefined it as a fun, counter-culture car. Advertising defined the experience and enhanced the enjoyment of it.

On a smaller level, a surprising ad might bring about the one unexpected smile someone experiences in a day.

If you go on to create advertising, or even approve it on the client side, I urge you to aim for something bigger. Yes, advertising needs to sell. But it can do so much more. It can create joy, beauty, laughter, and connections between people. Since we can't escape it, we should aim to use it to make a better world. Let's expect nothing less.

---

[81] Life Lessons from an Ad Man (2009) *TED*. [Online] Available from: https://www.ted.com/talks/rory_sutherland_life_lessons_from_an_ad_man [Accessed 20 January 2018].

THANK YOU!

The authors and Under One Hour, LLC thank you for your purchase. We truly hope you have found this publication valuable and will check out our other listings on our website here: www.UnderOneHour.com/Books

We are always looking to hear from our fans so if you liked the book, want to leave a comment, or give some feedback, contact us here: www.UnderOneHour.com/Contact-Us

Please sign up for our newsletter and follow our blog, Facebook, and Twitter to keep updated. We enjoy the interaction through all of these mediums, but feel free to use your favorite one.

If you would like to write your own Under One Hour book, please contact us on our author webpage: www.UnderOneHour.com/Write-For-UOH

Still included in this book are the **Bibliography,** and About the Author.

BIBLIOGRAPHY

I hope *Advertising Under One Hour* has inspired you to learn more about this exciting field. To help you achieve that goal, here are some additional books, magazines, and websites to get you started:

BOOKS

- **101 Things I Learned in Advertising School by Tracy Arrington with Matthew Fredrick, New York: Three Rivers Press, 2018**
- The Activation Imperative: How to Build Brands and Business by Inspiring Action by William Rosen and Laurence Minsky, Lanham, Maryland: Rowman & Littlefield, 2017
- Ad Critique: How to Deconstruct Ads in Order to Build Better Advertising by Nancy Tag, Los Angeles: Sage, 2012
- Advertising Campaign Planning: Developing an Advertising-based Marketing Plan by Jim Avery, Chicago: The Copy Workshop, 2000
- The Advertising Effect: How to Change Behavior by Adam Ferrier & Jennifer Fleming Victoria, Australia: Oxford University Press, 2014
- Advertising in America: The First Two Hundred Years by Charles A. Goodrum, New York: Harry N Abrams, 1990
- The Art of Client Service: 58 Things Every Advertising & Marketing Professional Should Know, Revised and Updated Edition by Robert Solomon, Chicago: Dearborn Trade Publishing, 2008
- Audio Branding: Using Sound to Build Your Brand by Laurence Minsky & Colleen Fahey, London: Kogan Page, 2017.
- Brand Builder Workbook by Pamela L. Mickelson, Chicago: The Copy Workshop, 2012
- The Business Side of Creativity: The Complete Guide to Running a Small Graphics Design or Communications Business (Third Updated Edition) by Cameron S. Foote, New York: W. W. Norton & Company, 2006
- Confessions of an Advertising Man by David Ogilvy, New York: Atheneum, 1963

- The Copy Workshop Workbook by Bruce Bendinger, Chicago: The Copy Workshop, 2009
- Creative Advertising: Ideas and Techniques from the World's Best Campaigns (New Edition) by Mario Pricken, London: Thames & Hudson, 2011
- Damn Good Advice (for People with Talent!) by George Lois New York: Phaidon, 2013
- Effective Advertising: Understanding When, How, and Why Advertising Works by Gerard J. Tellis, London: Sage, 2004
- Essentials of Advertising by Cluley, Robert, London: Kogan Page, 2017
- The Get A Job Workshop: How to Find Your Way to a Creative Career in Advertising, Branding, Collateral, Digital, Experiential & More by Laurence Minsky with contributions from 33 industry professionals, Chicago: The Copy Workshop, 2013
- Hey Whipple, Squeeze This! 5th Edition by Luke Sullivan & Edward Boches, New Jersey: John Wiley & Sons, 2016
- How to Succeed in Advertising When All You Have Is Talent Second Edition by Laurence Minsky, Chicago: The Copy Workshop, 2007
- Influence: Science and Practice 4th Edition by Robert Cialdini, Needham Heights, MA: Allyn & Bacon, 2001
- Juicing the Orange: How to Turn Creativity into a Powerful Business Advantage by Pat Fallon and Fred Senn, Boston, Massachusetts: Harvard Business School Press, 2006
- The Lost Diary of a Real Mad Man by Emerson Foote American Academy of Advertising, 2014
- Madison Avenue USA: The Extraordinary Business of Advertising and the People Who Run It by Martin Mayer, Lincolnwood, Illinois: NTC Business Books, 1992
- Ogilvy on Advertising by David Ogilvy, New York: Vintage Books, a Division of Random House, 1983
- Persuasive Advertising: Evidence-based Principles by J. Scott Armstrong, London: Palgrave Macmillan, 2010
- Reality in Advertising by Reeves, Rosser, New York: Alfred A. Knopf, 1985
- The Rise of Advertising in the United States: A History of Innovation to 1960 by Edd Applegate, Lanham, MD, Scarecrow Press, 2012
- Social Media Strategy: Marketing and Advertising in the Consumer Revolution by Keiyh A. Quesenberry, Lanham, Maryland: Rowman & Littlefield, 2016

- <u>A Technique for Producing Ideas</u> by James Webb Young, NTC Business Books, 1989
- <u>Thank You for Arguing: What Aristotle, Lincoln, and Homer Simpson Can Teach Us About the Art of Persuasion</u>, Third Edition by Jay Heinrichs, New York: Three Rivers Press, 2017
- <u>21 Days to a Big Idea: Creating Breakthrough Business Concepts</u> by Bryan Mattimore, Diversion Books, 2015
- <u>Whatever Happened to Madison Avenue: Advertising in the '90s</u> by Martin Mayer Boston, Massachusetts: Little Brown, 1991

KEY MAGAZINES, WEBSITES, AND INDUSTRY AWARD

- Ad Age
- Ad Busters
- Advertising Education Foundation
- Ad Week
- Andy Awards
- American Advertising Federation
- American Association of Advertising Agencies
- Association of National Advertisers
- Branding Magazine
- Business Insider/Advertising
- Campaign
- Cannes Lions
- Communication Arts
- Content Marketing Institute
- Cresta Awards
- Digiday
- The Drum
- Effie Awards
- Epica Awards
- Harvard Business Review
- Luerzers International Archive
- MarketingProfs

- Marketing Sherpa
- Marketing Week
- Media Post
- Mobius Awards
- The One Club **(See One Show Winners)**
- Path to Purchase Institute
- Post Control Marketing **(See Tools & Resources)**
- Print Magazine
- WARC

INDEX/KEY TERMS

Account Executive: 47, 49, 51, 52, 54
The Activation Imperative: 30, 54, 73
Agency Commission: 24
Art Director: 28, 54, 55, 57-61, 63, 65
Ayer, Francis W: 24
Barnum, P.T.: 25
Bezos, Jeff: 36
Blinkering: 73
Bogusky, Alex: 11, 30, 38, 58, 88
Brand Equity: 36
Briefing Process: 54
China: 21, 22
Copywriter: 5, 26-28, 54, 55, 57-59, 62, 63, 65
CPM/Cost Per Thousand: 71
Doyle Dane Bernbach/DDB: 28, 50, 63, 65, 90
Draper, Don: 28
Ethics: 39-42, 82
Facebook: 75
Fox: 70
Fraud: 78, 81
The General Date Protection Regulation (GDPR): 78
Graphic Designers: 58
Hopkins, Claude: 11, 27, 29, 34,
Instagram: 75
J Walter Thompson: 11, 50, 64, 81
King, Stephen: 50
LinkedIn: 75
Lord, Daniel: 26, 27
Magazines: 70, 74
McLuhan, Marshall: 8, 69,
Media Planner(s): 71-73
Media Studies: 55, 69
Middle Ages: 22
MSNBC: 70
Online Banner: 75, 76
Palmer, Volney B.: 24
PPC/Pay Per Click: 75, 78
Pollitt, Stanley: 50, 51
Positioning: 55, 82
Price: 24, 43, 46, 47, 71, 86
Production: 26, 57-59, 73, 74
Project Management: 58
Promotion: 30, 46
Push Advertising: 35
Rand, Paul: 11, 28, 63
Reality in Advertising: 41
Re-targeting: 77, 78
Research: 15, 25, 50, 51, 53, 57, 63, 71, 75, 81, 86

Account Planning: 49, 50, 52,
Advertising Plan: 25
Art Buyer: 59
Artificial Intelligence: 77
Banner Advertising: 75, 76
Bendinger, Bruce: 11, 31, 59, 96
Big Idea: 15, 29, 58
Boase Massimi Pollitt: 50
Brand Awareness: 75
Brief, Vreative: 39, 50, 54, 55, 63, 65, 73
Burnett, Leo: 11, 29-31, 48, 89
Cluley, Robert: 20
Creative Director: 28, 57, 64, 81
Egypt: 21
Experiential: 74
Flighting: 73
Franklin, Ben: 11, 23, 24, 29
Frequency: 72, 74
Halo Effect: 71
Hulu: 37
iPhone: 69
Journey Map: 77
Lasker, Albert: 11 ,26, 27, 29, 34
Lois, George: 11, 28
Mad Men: 15, 28, 89
Market Research: 15, 25, 71
Media Buyer(s): 76
Media Sales: 71
Newspapers: 22, 24, 25, 74
Mobile: 69, 70, 74, 75, 77
NW Ayer & Son: 24, 25, 29
Outdoor: 19, 70, 74, 76
Path-to Purchase: 77
Pinterest: 64, 75
Post-Campaign Analysis: 79, 82
Pre-emptive Advertising/Preemption: 27, 29
Primary Research: 53
Programmatic: 77, 78
Project Rate: 86,
Pull Advertising: 33
Radio: 19, 36, 38, 58, 70, 74, 76
Reach: 48, 71, 72, 74, 75, 78, 79
Re-marketing: 75
Reeves, Rosser: 11, 29, 30, 43, 44, 47

Richards, Stan: 11, 36, 84, 85
Secondary Research: 53
Soft Sell: 33, 37
Spec Work: 84
Strategy: 15, 22, 45, 47–51, 57, 63, 72, 77, 84
Sutherland, Rory: 11, 39, 90
TV Advertising: 76
Unique Selling Proposition/USP: 29, 30, 31, 47, 48, 54
Value Pricing: 86–87

Rome: 21
Social: 19, 24, 48, 70, 73–75, 77, 83
Song Dynasty: 22
Statement of Work (SOW): 88
Tactic: 39, 45, 84
Twitter: 75
4P's: 46

ABOUT THE AUTHOR

Laurence Minsky is renowned in both professional and academic circles for his strategic and creative leadership and his broad-reaching industry expertise which includes brand development, brand advertising, brand activation, content marketing, new product development, local store marketing, direct response, channel communications, and online and mobile marketing, as well as developing effective cross-channel solutions that boost overall marketing ROI.

He serves as an associate professor in the Department of Communication in the School of Media Arts at Columbia College Chicago and as a strategic and creative marketing consultant for leading agencies, corporations, and nonprofits across the globe.

Laurence is the co-author of The Activation Imperative: How to Build Brands and Business by Inspiring Action (Rowman & Littlefield, 2017), Audio Branding: Using Sound to Build Your Brand (Kogan Page 2017), executive editor of The Get A Job Workshop: How to Find Your Way to a Creative Career in Advertising, Branding, Collateral, Digital, Experiential & More (Copy Workshop, 2013), the author of How to Succeed in Advertising When All You Have Is Talent Second Edition (Copy Workshop 2007) and coauthor of Advertising and the Business of Brands Media Revolution Edition (Copy Workshop 2009). As an industry thought-leader, he has been published by the Harvard Business Review, European Business Review, MarketingProfs, and the Data-Driven Marketing Network, and has been quoted in the New York Times, Chicago Tribune, Chicago Sun-Times, San Diego Union Tribune,

Exame (Brazil's largest business and economics magazine), Shopify's blog, and Crain's Chicago Business, among many others.

His agency experience includes a tenure at Frankel (now Arc Worldwide) and engagements with more than 25 other agencies as a consultant. And, he has created strategic and communications solutions for many blue-chip clients, including AARP, Laila Ali, Amazon, Ambius, AON, Bay Valley Foods, Beltone, Black & Decker Spacemaker, Bristol-Myers Squibb, Coca-Cola, Connie's Pizza, Encyclopaedia Britannica, Fleetwood Homes, Frito-Lay, George Foreman Products, Kraft Foods, The Lakeside Collection, Lamin-Art, Mayo Medical Laboratories (Mayo Clinic), McDonald's, Midtown Athletic Clubs, Motorola, Naples Bay Resort, PetSmart, Spacelabs Healthcare, Taiwan External Trade Development Council (TAITRA), True Value, Unilever, United Airlines, United States Postal Service, Westinghouse, Vita Foods, and more.

An award-winning creative with more than 125 industry accolades to date, he has served on the juries of many leading industry award shows, including Lürzer's International Archive 200 Best Digital Artists Worldwide 2015/2016, The One Show Young Ones Competition, and the Design of the Times, and he is a long-standing member of the One Club for Art and Copy, the Authors Guild, and the American Academy of Advertising.

"Years of experience by a seasoned advertising guru that you can grasp in the time it takes to do a business lunch."

— Thomas McManus, Associate Professor, Fashion Institute of Technology